Fast Feedback

Other titles from Bloomsbury Education

The Wellbeing Toolkit: Sustaining, supporting and enabling school staff by Andrew Cowley

What Works?: Research and evidence for successful teaching by Lee Elliot Major and Steve Higgins

Teaching Rebooted: Using the science of learning to transform classroom practice by Jon Tait

The Headteacher's Handbook: The essential guide to leading a primary school by Rae Snape

The Inclusive Classroom: A new approach to differentiation by Daniel Sobel and Sara Alston

Fast Feedback

How one primary school abolished written marking

Lesley Hill with
Gemma Whitby

Foreword by Matthew Kleiner-Mann

BLOOMSBURY EDUCATION
LONDON OXFORD NEW YORK NEW DELHI SYDNEY

BLOOMSBURY EDUCATION
Bloomsbury Publishing Plc
50 Bedford Square, London, WC1B 3DP, UK
29 Earlsfort Terrace, Dublin 2, Ireland

BLOOMSBURY, BLOOMSBURY EDUCATION and the Diana logo are trademarks of Bloomsbury Publishing Plc

First published in Great Britain, 2022
This edition published in Great Britain, 2022

A catalogue record for this book is available from the British Library

ISBN: PB: 978-1-8019-9001-1; ePDF: 978-1-8019-9003-5; ePub: 978-1-8019-9002-8

2 4 6 8 10 9 7 5 3 1 (paperback)

Typeset by Newgen KnowledgeWorks Pvt. Ltd., Chennai, India
Printed and bound in the UK by CPI Group Ltd, CR0 4YY

Contents

Acknowledgements

Thanks from Lesley

My heartfelt thanks and gratitude:

To Libby Lee, who suggested that I write a book about Fast Feedback.

To Matthew, for never losing interest in the idea (and not minding my brutal honesty).

To Natasha, for working to get it noticed.

To Hannah and Lucy at Bloomsbury, for believing in the idea and helping us to get it right.

To the theorists, educationalists and all the adults and pupils at Lavender School (and beyond), without whom there would be no story.

To all the former colleagues who gave their time to share memories and examples.

To Haeun, for sharing her tremendous talent and creativity, and for being so patient with me.

To my wonderful family (especially my husband Ash) and my dear friends, for always supporting and encouraging me, whatever adventure I decide to go on.

And finally, of course:

To Gemma, whose commitment and utter brilliance meant that this book could happen.

Thanks from Gemma

Firstly, I would like to thank Matthew and Lavender for the many opportunities you have given me, including writing this book, and Hannah and Lucy at Bloomsbury for your valuable feedback and friendly guidance during this process.

I would also like to thank the dedicated, inspiring and supportive colleagues I have had the privilege of working with over the years. I hope that this book will help you to achieve the work–life balance you deserve.

To my family, especially my husband Mike: thank you for your unwavering support and understanding, particularly when it comes to workload. And to my children; should you ever wish to become teachers, I hope that I can only respond with pride and encouragement!

Finally, to Lesley: it has been a pleasure writing this with you. Your support has been incredible and I have loved working with you again. Thank you for thinking of me.

Foreword

How do you ensure that children are learning, without bringing staff to their knees? We found a way.

Six years ago, I decided to ban teachers from writing in children's books. Children became more independent, the quality of their writing improved and standards went up. Ofsted are happy with it and, crucially, so are teachers. Since then, 'no marking' has really caught on. Over the last few years, there have been blogs, tweets and articles aplenty about changes to reduce teacher workload and to improve retention.

In the summer of 2016, Lavender and Brimsdown Primary Schools successfully introduced Fast Feedback. Since then, our schools have held many conferences and provided countless training sessions on elements of 'no marking'. However, the journey to this success was complex, and involved a range of policy change, besides just the one about marking.

This book shares that journey through Lavender's story. It is a tale of ups and downs, and of real-life primary practice. But it is also a guide, which will support you should you decide to establish the approach within your own schools. Lesley's honest storytelling is interwoven with theoretical contributions from Gemma, examples of practice from other schools, and useful questions and tips.

The authors, both former teachers and leaders at Lavender, worked tirelessly alongside the whole staff team to guarantee the success of my vision.

Of course, you may already lead or teach in a no-marking school, in which case I hope that aspects of our journey will resonate with you, help you in some way and possibly even make you laugh.

Enjoy.

Matthew (CEO, Ivy Learning Trust)

Introduction

During my teaching career I have felt rewarded beyond measure, but I have also felt totally, utterly exhausted. My hope for this book is that it will support you in your own efforts to reduce teacher exhaustion and to help children become truly effective learners. It is written for teachers *and* school leaders (at any level) but it is not a simple 'how to guide'. I truly believe that initiatives should not be introduced in a tick-list fashion: schools have different starting points, experiences and needs. So, the 'how to' is shared within a true tale, adding context and depth, so that you can consider how it might work in your own setting.

Nevertheless, depending on where you are in your no-marking journey, you may wish to use just certain elements as a guide, dipping in and out of the theory, focusing only on the tips or skipping a chapter or two, and that is fine – I have outlined where you'll find the guiding points below. However, I warmly encourage you to read the *story*. It lays bare our mistakes and celebrates our successes. It explains why we do what we do, and knowing about our journey, the good and the bad, will help you to make Fast Feedback your own. Also, because I've aimed to keep the story light and honest, hopefully you'll be entertained too!

'How to' quickly access the 'how to'

Fact files

Gemma's fact files, throughout the book, expand on the educational theories and pedagogy drawn upon in the story. They are about the people and ideas that influenced our decision-making at the time and which we feel are important to making Fast Feedback work. This doesn't mean that we expect you to slavishly follow a particular theory (just as we wouldn't!) but we hope that a mention or reminder of those names and their messages will support you in your own no-marking journey. Much of the theory we feature is, of course, well known and is there for 'recap' if wanted, or to skip entirely if you choose. If you would like more, Gemma has provided the names of a few relevant texts that may be of interest. The 'putting it into practice' tips in this section, gleaned from both teachers and leaders, will be extremely useful if you are at the point of introducing or embedding those elements of our Fast Feedback approach.

Quick questions

At key points in each chapter, you will find a food-for-thought question. These questions are here simply as triggers for you to contemplate and reflect on your own or on your school's practice.

Quick tips

Every now and then I offer a tip or two around an aspect of Fast Feedback. The rationale behind each of the tips will be made clear within the story, but you may find them useful as reminders when developing the Fast Feedback approach.

Chapter summaries

Chapters 2–7 conclude with a quick summary of the key messages contained within them so that you can dip back in to support your introduction of Fast Feedback. You will also find a bullet-point summary of the Fast Feedback approach at the beginning of Chapter 7.

1 Waking up to workload *Where it all started*

The case of misunderstanding

'Going anywhere nice?'

A quizzical face came back at him, so Matthew gestured towards the suitcase.

'Oh! No, unfortunately. This is my marking for the weekend.'

It was December 2013 and Matthew Kleiner-Mann was determined to be a great headteacher. He insisted on the best for his children, he embraced innovation and he was passionate about staff development.

Being a great headteacher meant modelling a good work–life balance so, as it was 4.30 pm on a Friday, he was going home. Weekend time with the family beckoned and he only had the tiniest twinge of guilt for leaving some Lavender Primary School teachers and leaders behind.

It so happened that he ended up walking out with a Year 2 teacher – a brilliant NQT (now known as 'early career teacher') whom he'd been delighted to employ that year as it was becoming increasingly difficult to secure teachers. He was surprised that Nicola was leaving so early as she usually had to be encouraged out by a site manager at lock-up time.

Matthew was surprised but delighted – his modelling was working, and he now had no reason to feel that teeny guilt twinge. Noticing that Nicola was pulling a rather smart wheely suitcase behind her, he made polite conversation and asked that question. No, the suitcase was not for a wonderful weekend away. It was to carry work.

Ooh, we Lavender teachers loved our wheels back then. Like a craze sweeps through the playground, so 'teacher wheels' swept through the staff room. One that really caught on was a collapsible box contraption that came in no end of bright colours; best prices and suppliers were shared avidly. Some teachers, like Nicola, used a trusty wheeled weekend case with a retractable handle. I went retro with a pull-along shopping bag, at which a friend laughed and mumbled the words 'old lady'.

I wasn't convinced that it was my trolley design, but rather the actual use of a wheeled item that was so amusing to her. I can't deny being a bit short when I explained that it was important for us teachers to protect our backs. I suppose I was irritated that she didn't seem to realise how bad our workload was.

Quick Question: Do teachers at your school have wheely cases, or similar, for their books?

Matthew's Friday drive home was different that week. Usually, he would be planning for the family weekend ahead but that afternoon he had to process what had just happened. The more he processed, the more images came flooding in. Teacher after teacher pulling along cases. Not just on Fridays either. He'd seen it on weekday evenings too. Late. At lock-up time. He pictured Nicola, a fresh-faced, eager NQT skipping into school in September and, within a term, worn out, exhausted and dragging her work behind her. Teachers – worn out, exhausted and dragging their wheels behind them. No wonder teachers were leaving the profession. It was well documented and so was the reason.

A 2016–17 House of Commons Education Committee (2017) report on recruitment and retention highlighted that the number of teachers leaving the profession rose by 11 per cent between 2011 and 2014. The most common reason given was workload. The report also highlights that a shocking 76 per cent of newly qualified teacher (NQT) respondents to an ATL survey said that they had considered leaving teaching precisely because of workload.

'Who'd want to be a teacher? They don't have a life,' Matthew found himself saying aloud. That twinge of momentary guilt for leaving early became heavier as he realised that he was responsible. He'd caused this, and to understand how, I need to take you back to 2009 – four years before the suitcase incident.

Data reaction

One day in the summer term of 2009, I spent close to three hours in a minibus with a teacher from the local secondary school. We were driving down to the south coast, where the Year 6 children were on a residential trip. His job was to bring back some pupils so that they could attend an induction day.

My job was to take some news to Matthew that shouldn't be shared over the phone.

I tried to show polite interest in the lane-change strategy for traffic avoidance tips and other conversation, but a little voice inside just kept saying, 'Twenty-four per cent. Twenty-four per cent.' My job was to share with Matthew his first set of SATs data as a headteacher.

Lavender Primary School got the lowest writing results in the borough.

It is true.

(I expect you may now have an urge to ditch this book. Why on earth would you want to take advice and tips from an organisation that has failed so miserably!? Please don't worry. Stay with me. It got better – much better.)

Our other data wasn't great either, but our writing results were truly shocking. Actually, I will take this opportunity to send a little hug of understanding to all the Year 6 teachers out there. It's a hard job, made harder by the fact that you're working to get your children on or above track, regardless of the learning experiences they've had over the last five or six years.

Now, I was one of the Year 6 teachers that year and I was well placed to understand what had happened and was certainly well placed to take some blame. At the time I looked for ways to blame others too, but I won't discuss that here – it is in the past. It was a horrible time. It was a horrible message to share, and I'll never forget Matthew's reaction; his state of shock and disbelief. I have to say I learned my biggest leadership lesson that afternoon.

Quick Tip: As a headteacher, be ready to deal with some real crap.

After that terrible news, the school went into overdrive. We trawled through every paper and questioned every mark with a ridiculous and desperate belief that even just one more child scraping a pass would redeem us somehow. It didn't, of course. The local authority school improvement partner (SIP) came in and helped form a disaster recovery plan. There was an emergency governors' meeting, which I could describe as difficult but that doesn't even come close. The whole school, teachers and TAs, went to a swish theatre in the West

End to hear Ros Wilson explain her Big Writing scheme. The local authority sent in consultants, and leaders and teachers from other schools. Staff were shifted across year groups and sent on every bit of training available. In-house training was intense and focused. Writing became the most important subject in school and there needed to be MORE! It all got a little manic for a while, and whilst the Year 2 programme MFW stood for 'More Fabulous Writing', I have inside knowledge that sometimes the Fabulous got replaced.

Another thing that happened was the 'Big Writing expectations' document.

We'd always had literacy policies, naturally, and we were also developing a fabulous 'Teaching and Learning Policy'. However, writing now warranted its very own document. Over the following years, the expectations for Big Writing became more and more detailed and more and more prescriptive.

Success criteria

In the beginning, we dutifully set out success criteria for the children using the Must, Should and Could method that was so popular back then. Teachers used the learning intention to create three bands of hierarchical success criteria, and the children would regulate themselves as they saw fit. The idea was that the children who were struggling would work to achieve the *must*, whereas the higher achievers would complete the *must* without much effort, sail happily through the *should* and then challenge themselves with the *could*.

With the smugness that comes with so much staff training and development came the misled opinion that we were doing the very best for our children, but, as a Year 2 teacher at that time, I struggled. I found it so difficult to rank writing success criteria, and that added hours to planning time. What usually happened was that the 'must' column became a list of mechanical skills such as 'use a full stop at the end of a sentence' and 'spell tricky words correctly'. The last column delved deeper with such criteria as 'describe how (insert character name) might be feeling and why.' There was a problem with this, of course; we all know those children who can say it but can't write it. B could most definitely explain how a character was feeling, and why, but I'd be damned if he ever put a full stop anywhere in his writing.

Our naivety was short-lived, thank goodness, and it only took a bit of reading and some great training sessions from the likes of Pie Corbett, Shirley Clarke and others to realise the nonsense of hierarchical success criteria and that all elements of a particular genre are important. Read more on how to get this right in this chapter's fact file on success criteria.

FACT FILE: SUCCESS CRITERIA

What

Success criteria are a breakdown of steps or ingredients to enable the learner to meet the learning objective so that pupils know what is expected of them and when they have achieved it.

Why success criteria are important to Fast Feedback

When children mark their own work, as part of our Fast Feedback approach, it is essential that they understand what they are marking against. The success criteria given must be clear and understood by the children, i.e. created with them, to ensure they are best placed to self-mark and to give effective peer feedback.

Key people

- Shirley Clarke – international freelance consultant leading courses, conducting research and writing books about the power of formative assessment (Clarke, 2008; 2021).
- Pie Corbett – educational trainer, author and creator of the 'Talk for Writing' approach to learning (Corbett, 2021).

- John Hattie – researcher in education and proponent of evidence-based teaching; well known for his books on 'Visible Learning' (Hattie, 2009; 2012).

Key messages

Clarke – success criteria should be:

- Seen as a move from product to process – pupils need to know what the final outcome should look like, but also the steps or ingredients needed to be successful.
- Known in basic form by teachers first, used across the curriculum and constantly referred to.
- The same for *all* learners – not hierarchical.
- Co-constructed with pupils and derived from analysing excellent examples, to have more meaning and impact on learning.
- Decontextualised and generic for applied skills so that they are transferable to any context.

These can be:

Compulsory closed skills	**Optional open toolkits**
- Steps that *must* be included to be successful. - The learning intention is achieved once the criteria are mastered. - Begin with 'remember to…'. - For maths or grammar skills.	- A menu of possibilities that *could* be included but not all are needed to be successful. - Seeing what excellence looks like is key. - Begin with 'choose from…'. - For a fictional piece of writing.

(Shirley Clarke Education, 2021b)

Hattie – success criteria should:

- Tell pupils what they are supposed to *learn*, not what they are supposed to do – it's not about the task.
- Equip pupils with the tools to be able to self- and peer-assess.
- Not just be shared with pupils: they must be *involved* in making it to keep them engaged in and enjoying the challenge of learning.
- Come from an end product or model and be taught upfront to provide direction, so that they can see what success looks like and will know when they get there (Hattie, 2012).

Corbett – success criteria and the 'Talk for Writing' approach:

Success criteria are also essential in Corbett's writing process, where learners move from imitation to innovation to invention (independent application).

- *Imitation* – pupils analyse a quality model text pitched above their level. They identify structures and language patterns and use these to co-construct a toolkit. Criteria must encourage children to think like writers and consider the effect upon the reader.
- *Innovation* – pupils co-construct new versions of the text with their teacher using the ingredients.
- *Invention* – pupils create their own original texts. Over time, they can internalise and select appropriate features automatically, no longer needing a visual support to scaffold their writing (Corbett, 2021).

Are success criteria always effective?

Durran – 'boxed' or 'expanding success criteria'

- James Durran, a former teacher and now local authority adviser, argues that using a checklist of features or ticking off specific ingredients does not define success and can be limiting.
- Durran believes that writing should be seen as writing: a whole text with a purpose, written for the intended reader, and richness and variety should be valued.
- Durran developed 'boxed' or 'expanded success criteria' as an alternative to listed success criteria. The ingredients are still there but are linked to audience, intended effect on the audience and vocabulary choices (see further reading, Durran, 2019) .

Putting it into practice

For leaders

- Give teachers the opportunity to share best practice for co-constructing success criteria across the key stages during regular meetings.
- Provide training for all new staff and ensure they have the opportunity to work alongside peers in order to support and embed their understanding of the techniques.

For teachers

Tips for co-constructing success criteria

- Ensure success criteria focus on the purpose of the writing and effect on the reader rather than on grammatical features.

- Ensure 'process' success criteria are used to give pupils or teachers something to assess against.
- Analyse quality model texts as a class (teacher-made or anonymous examples from previous years) that include everything you hope to see, and identify the language structures – for example, ask children to independently extract examples from the text and record them in a table under each feature.
- Put a deconstructed text back together to identify the structural features and layout (this works particularly well with non-fiction texts).
- Use a visualiser to highlight examples of the success criteria in children's work.
- Use 'washing lines' to display success criteria and scribed writing.
- Don't write learning intentions or success criteria on the board before the lesson starts if it could reduce interest or give away too much.
- Compare an excellent example with a poor example to uncover the differences or improve poor-quality success criteria (see further reading, Shirley Clarke, 2021 for more techniques for generating success criteria).

Using toolkits to assess

- Keep criteria short, succinct and focused.
- Have the first toolkit item as a focus on the children's personal target (to support them to internalise it) or as mechanical skills.
- Number success criteria so children can easily identify the features in their writing and number them in the margin when assessing their work.

- For independent or assessment pieces, children could create their own toolkits based on what they have learned.

Key quote

'When teachers simply give students success criteria, they can be hard to interpret and are often ignored. When students have come up with them by a particularly rich co-construction strategy, they tend to remember them and internalise them.' (Clarke, 2021, p. 9)

Further reading

- Clarke, S. (2021), *Unlocking Learning Intentions and Success Criteria*. USA: Corwin.

  (Clarke's most recent publication, for more strategies on co-constructing success criteria)
- Durran, J. (2019), Re-thinking 'success criteria': A simple device to support pupils' writing, https://jamesdurran.blog/2019/01/24/re-thinking-success-criteria-a-simple-device-to-support-pupils-writing

  (For more information about and examples of 'boxed' or 'expanding success criteria')
- Corbett, P. (2021), Talk for Writing resources, www.talk4writing.com/resources

  (Free videos and resources to support teachers and children to generate criteria and write toolkits; particularly helpful for narratives)
- Shirley Clarke Education (2021b), Transforming learning through formative assessment, www.shirleyclarke-education.org

  (Video clips of teachers in action, access to lessons, a collection of useful websites and publications and case studies supporting formative assessment)

The path to success

So, based on the ideas of Clarke and Corbett the toolkit was introduced. Unlike hierarchical success criteria, the toolkit is a selection of ingredients that are all essential to a successful piece of writing. The first ingredient would be the child's own target, if relevant (use full stops at the end of a sentence wouldn't be applicable to writing poetry, of course). Creating the toolkit 'with' the children is important and you can find out more about doing that through text deconstruction in the fact file on success criteria. (You can also find a link to Durran's (2019) brilliant ideas around the 'boxed' or 'expanding' success criteria approach, which puts the audience at the centre of a piece of writing.) Using toolkits helped children to better fashion their pieces as well as being an important step in our Fast Feedback journey: the ticking of toolkit items *by children themselves*, which was included in our new and improved Big Writing expectations, set them on the path to marking their own work. You can see an example of this in Figure 1.1, which also shows how the child has carried out a follow-up task after self-marking. Don't worry, the numbering is not hierarchical but there to use as a reference when the child highlights examples in their writing.

The full Big Writing expectations were set out in a beautifully crafted document, with coloured illustrations and examples, so that every teacher knew what to do. We (OK, I) even wrote the words 'green pen' in green to make sure that a rogue marking pen didn't make its way into the books.

The actual Big Writing event was designed to be a wondrous experience. Teachers would guide children carefully towards the final writing task by creating highly strategic literacy planning. The value of talk, as recommended by Ros Wilson through her Big Writing approach, was well understood, so we included a 'Big Talk' homework session the night before. We recognised that not every child would experience that delightful family chat, so we met the need by providing in-school, adult-supported talk homework.

	I am learning to write a diary entry	Me	My friend
1	First person *I felt a tender kiss on my cheek*	✓	✓
2	Thoughts and feelings *I felt calm and peaceful*	✓	✓
3	Past tense I *sat surrounded* by the darkness	✓	✓
4	Description of what is happening *Sitting at the piano...* *Touching the keys...*	✓	✓
5	Range of sentence starters (fronted adverbials) *As the music became sweeter,* *Gradually,*	✓	✓
6	Structure and layout of a diary entry *Dear diary, date, paragraphs*	✓	✓

War Scene:
* At this moment, I didn't want to move; I was shocked.

Figure 1.1 *The examples in this toolkit (in italics) enabled the child to not only mark their own work but to also make improvements to the piece.*

> **Quick Question: Do your pupils get a chance to talk about their writing before they write?**

Even the atmosphere for writing was directed: we demanded music, dimmed lighting and visual focal points. So how did this go? Originally, we'd had real candles on tables but the health and safety discussions about them at governor meetings became wearisome, so some teachers went for trippy whiteboard visuals or some lava lamps and others just got those funny little battery-operated candles instead. What about the music? Well, I'd imagined that everyone would play some beautiful background piano music, such as Einaudi or Satie, but learning walks proved me wrong. I really did witness a Big Writing session accompanied by Beethoven's 5th – at volume.

Making a mark

We had the preparation and we had the mood. We also made it perfectly clear what the teacher should be doing after the session, with… and now we're coming to it… very specific guidance on how to mark the work. The actual document, in full glorious colour, is long, so here it is for you in a (rather large) nutshell:

Green pen to correct (certain) spelling/punctuation errors.
Yellow pen to highlight where a child has met a toolkit item.
Green pen to cross-reference/number the toolkit item met.
Pink pen to highlight a successful paragraph.
Green pen to write a positive comment. Leave a space.
Green pen to write a next step. Leave a space.
Green pen to set a response task specific to next step above.
Choose words for spelling journal – don't care what colour pen you use here.
Red pen for children to carry out response task.
Green pen to mark response task.
Red pen for children doing work during conference marking.*
Green pen to mark work during conference marking.*
Green pen to label conference marking 'conference marked'.*

**In case you're wondering, as well as marking at home, teachers were allowed to 'conference' mark a group of children in the classroom now and then – this was a true forerunner to our Fast Feedback approach.*

I can't remember the suppliers we used then but when we found out that they did double-ended highlighter pens, one end pink and the other yellow, we were in stationery heaven. It became almost fashionable to have streaks of yellow and pink up and down your forearms. It was like warpaint; like you'd been in a battle and overcome the enemy.

Big Writing happened on a Thursday morning for Key Stage 2, whereas Key Stage 1 was on a Friday (the little ones needed a longer delivery of the unit), so Nicola and her colleagues benefited from having the whole weekend to do their Big Marking (yay).

Obviously, Key Stage 2 had to get their marking done and dusted so that the children could do their response tasks on Friday morning.

Now, as Matthew was determined to be a great headteacher, he persuaded the site managers to keep the school open late on Thursdays. An agreement was made that teachers wouldn't be encouraged to leave until 7.00 pm to enable them to do their 'Big Marking'.

This whole nonsense went on for years.

Quick Question: How many hours a week do teachers at your school spend writing in children's books?

Ask Matthew now who was to blame for that marking misery, and he will take a share. The 2009 results demanded it. He demanded it. He would task his leaders to rewrite policies over and over to make them 'clearer', to make them 'better', to 'ensure better results for the children'. (Yes, leaders suffered from workload stress as well.) But he blames others too, namely Ofsted and the local authority, for the messages he received. Lavender was due another Ofsted visit. We'd done all right in 2012; all the work we'd put in place, following the 'you know what' results, was paying off. We were officially a good school with some outstanding bits, which was nice, thank you very much. However, we knew we were worth more. Our hard work and smugness compelled us to strive for an outstanding judgement, so advice was sought. Local authority experts came in chanting, 'It's about the books. It's all about the books.' That meant (to us) that marking had to be super-detailed and, by default, super-colourful. Ofsted talked about feedback. That meant (to us) that marking had to be super-detailed and, by default, written.

Quick Tip: Don't design your policies for Ofsted, design them for children's learning.

From the mouths of babes

Although Matthew had had a wheely-case wake-up call four years into the suffering caused by this crazy policy, it was another two years before his daughter Sacha really opened his eyes to the fact that something needed to be done.

In the summer term of 2015, as part of the effort to secure collaboration with another group of schools, we attended a strategy meeting. By then, we were a pair of schools and I'd made it to acting head. Following successful support work with failing schools in the borough, Matthew had been invited to take on the leadership of Brimsdown Primary School as executive head (for there's nothing like your own successful recovery to qualify you to recover others). We were exploring academisation and, along with executives and heads from other schools, we sat around a table to discuss how, as a trust, we might tackle recruitment and retention problems.

Recruitment was a big issue then and sometimes got a little dirty. Attending Schools Direct interviews put leaders into competition with one another to try to secure the best of the bunch. It sometimes reached the realm of ridiculous when trying to persuade a candidate that your school was the one that they should choose. I remember being *so* close to winning over a potentially brilliant trainee teacher, when another head snuck in with the remark, 'Well, we've got a goat!' Farm animals aside, we had worked quite creatively at Lavender to attract and keep teachers (you can skip ahead to the last chapter to read more on that), but there was no doubt that, nationally, the profession was suffering.

It was at this meeting that Matthew told us about the conversation with his eight-year-old daughter, Sacha. She had said to him the words that no parent would want to hear from their child at that time. She had said, 'Daddy, when I grow up, I want to be a teacher.'

It was at this meeting that Matthew shared his idea to solve the recruitment crisis. The suitcase experience from years before had never left him. He knew he'd done something wrong and he wanted to put it right. Let me just mention something here: Matthew wasn't the sort of leader who would do things in a half-hearted way. There was no 'perhaps we should cut down on marking expectations' (he thought that would look lazy), it was full steam ahead with:

'Let's abolish marking. Let's get the children to mark their own work.'

We all tried to be professional and stick to some sort of meeting protocol, but everyone was too animated. It was daring. It was risky. It was exciting.

I was especially excited because children marking their own work fitted so well with a mission we'd been on for years. My passion for developing children as agents of their own learning was forefront in my own pedagogy and practice. I knew, as did Matthew, that children at Lavender were ready to take on responsibility for their own work. I knew that the journey we'd taken had put them in the right place.

So, we banned teacher marking. No writing in children's books, on their homework, in their reading records, on their artwork, nothing – not even a sticker. It was big, it was life-changing and it works. Now you can share in our journey and see how each step we took was important to the success of what came to be called Fast Feedback. There is no single template for how to introduce the approach. There is our story and there are examples of how other settings have adapted elements. However, there is one truth:

With the wrong culture, banning marking could be a disaster. But with the right culture, the impact is transformative.

2 The way we were *Creating an ethos for learning*

Values and behaviour

So, what is the right culture? How did we know that our children were ready to mark their own work? First, let's talk about ethos.

Did you ever walk into a school, as a visitor, and not really like it or feel uncomfortable? Conversely, have you ever walked into a school and just loved it? Often, the reasons are intangible – a gut feeling you get (the whole idea of gut feeling and thin-slicing is fascinating; if you've not read Malcolm Gladwell's (2006) thoughts around these topics, then you're missing out!). I firmly believe that you can create a feel-good school through the decisions and actions you take as a teacher, leader or indeed any staff member. One of Matthew's first decisions as a new headteacher at Lavender was to sort out behaviour. It wasn't great. There were many delightful children who would never put a foot wrong. There were also some for whom the 'F word' was acceptable language to use when inviting a teacher to leave the room. But the majority fell somewhere in between; they needed guidance and boundaries… and maybe something else.

The new behaviour policy turned things around. The beauty of it was that it wasn't purely a list of rewards and sanctions; it was a template for creating respect between all members of the school community. We all know how busy the school day can get and how easy it is to have your sights focused solely on getting the next bit of planning done or the next lot of resources ready (or just getting to the loo before someone shouts 'They're in!'). One rule of the behaviour policy was: 'All adults should smile and acknowledge children as they pass by.'

Simple?

Or genius?

Matthew modelled this and it didn't take long to catch on. It was refreshing. One of the delights of being at Lavender, indeed at any Ivy school, is having children smile and not just say hello, but ask you how you are, ask you if you're having a nice day. It feels good when you walk through the door.

Quick Question: Does your behaviour policy actively encourage positive interactions between all?

A couple of years later, we also introduced our core values and as they, like the behaviour policy, applied to both children and staff, everyone was involved in choosing them.

Quick Tip: If you are reviewing your school vision and values, find a way to include all stakeholders.

It was a complicated system of voting, justifying and narrowing but we ended up with six: Care, Responsibility, Determination, Respect, Friendship and Honesty. The children designed characters to represent each value and the values were portrayed and embedded around the school. (Just in case you visit and can't find Mr Friendship now, he announced in a whole-school assembly a few years back that he'd officially changed his name to Mr Appreciation. Mr Care had taken over his duties and he now had a new job description.) Now, of course, there are also the British Values.

Lavender's behaviour policy refers very specifically to the values. If children do something wrong, they must consider which value they are not following. During the weekly Achievement Assemblies, children are awarded for going above and beyond when showing a particular value.

There was even a Lavender Values song written by the children with the help of the wonderful George and Christalla of Musical Playground (which you can find on their YouTube account).

But the values were not just about improving social behaviour and ethos. Some became critical when we introduced Fast Feedback: children needed to take a great deal of responsibility for their own learning, take care in their work and show determination when striving to get better. Respect for one another was essential when children were giving feedback on one another's work (they would also need to be very honest about how they were doing, and we'll come to that in a bit).

Quick Question: Do your school values apply to learning as well as to social behaviour?

Hands-down policy

So, we knew that our values supported our no-marking approach, as did our 'no-hands-up' policy. The idea of the policy was to help to embed assessment for learning, but it was also meant to eliminate the hands-up nonsense. We knew from reading and experience that it was nonsense because…

There were the children who always put their hand up because they knew the answer, thought they knew the answer or just wanted to speak. The 'hand up' was usually accompanied by an 'ooh, ooh!' noise – a sort of desperate 'pick me' signal – and the teacher's common response would be '… and I won't be picking anyone making silly noises' (the child would then pull an equally 'desperate to be picked' face instead).

There were also the children who would put up their hand even though they didn't know the answer (or *thought* that they didn't know the answer) but wanted to try to contribute, and maybe look like they knew the answer. These children would have a sort of half-hearted, elbow no higher than the shoulder, one finger 'hands-up' style.

Then there were the children who did not want to be picked at all. They put up their hand because they'd learned that the teacher would often pick the children who *didn't* have their hands up! They were playing a very strategic hands-up game.

We'd worked hard to implement assessment for learning (AFL) across the school: Shirley Clarke's book, *Active Learning Through Formative Assessment* (Clarke, 2008), had been purchased in bulk and we had a 'no-hands-up' policy to die for, with cups in colours, smiley and not-so-smiley faces, thumbs up, thumbs down, thumbs in the middle and, of course … lolly-sticks.

Using the stick is simple:

The teacher asks a question and allows some thinking time.

The children discuss their thoughts with a partner.

Everyone is ready to contribute when a named lolly-stick is picked.

To ensure that every child was picked at some point during a session, the teacher would put picked sticks aside. Needless to say, children soon cottoned on to the fact that they could relax after they'd been named, and some teachers had to resort to rather 'creative' stick picking (you know how it is). The teacher would then have a good idea of each child's understanding to inform their teaching.

Quick Question: How do teachers at your school ensure all children are actively engaged? How do they know?

Essential to this was the use of talk partners. We'd had talk partners established for some time, and research helped us to make the strategy more effective by including regular partner swaps and peer reviews of partner skills. This also stood us in good stead to introduce our Fast Feedback approach, of which cooperative reviews became an integral part (you can read more about this in Chapter 6).

Effective questioning

I have to admit now that talk partner work wasn't always effective. During more observations as a leader than I'd care to remember, I saw the talk partner strategy lead to pairs of children madly shouting words or numbers into each other's faces. You probably know exactly what has happened here. The teacher has asked a closed question.

Questioning was a key element of our lolly-stick approach (indeed, it had to be! One of our Ofsted areas for development was to 'make effective use of questioning'). One memorable staff meeting had us using Bloom's Taxonomy to pull apart fairy tales until we were truly analysing, evaluating and creating havoc (our INSETs always have a fun element). We learned about different types of questions, how to ask open questions, how to encourage higher-order thinking (HOT) and that even closed questions can be HOT. (What colour *is* the sky anyway?) Of course, that's not to say that questions to assess factual recall aren't important; they most certainly are, especially when you're delivering a knowledge-based curriculum.

Quick Tip: Teachers can film themselves teaching a session, watch themselves and do a tally of the types of questions they ask.

Effective questioning for partner work, however, is key if you want a bit more thinking and exploring of ideas to go on. You can read more on Bloom and others' ideas around types of questions in this fact file on effective questioning.

FACT FILE: EFFECTIVE QUESTIONING

What

Questioning is the most common form of interaction in the classroom: it engages students in the learning process, challenges their thinking and can be a powerful tool for assessing and developing learning.

Why effective questioning is important to Fast Feedback

Through effective questioning, which challenges their thinking, children begin to understand that there isn't necessarily just a yes or no answer to a question. They learn that questions can lead to collaborative discussion and exploration, which helps to prepare them for peer evaluations. They begin to see that learning can involve a deeper level of thinking and will be encouraged to ask questions themselves, and of themselves, promoting reflection and metacognition – essential if they are to take control of their own learning as part of the Fast Feedback approach.

Key people

Benjamin Bloom

Bloom was an educational psychologist who is well known for his book *Taxonomy of Educational Objectives* (1956). This work was later revised by Lorin Anderson and David Krathwohl in 2001.

Key messages

Bloom's Taxonomy

- Bloom developed a framework for categorising educational goals according to their complexity.
- The cognitive domain comprised six thinking levels in a hierarchy, ordered from simple to complex: knowledge, comprehension, application, analysis, synthesis and evaluation.
- There should be cumulative mastery of one level before the next.
- The aim was to shift the focus away from content and instruction and encourage higher-order forms of thinking that focus on depth of learning rather than basic knowledge retention.
- Bloom's framework has since been revised to make it more relevant, dynamic and easier for teachers to implement.

Bloom's Revised Framework (Anderson and Krathwohl, 2001)

- **Remembering** – recall facts and basic concepts e.g. define, list, identify, memorise, recite, label

- **Understanding** – explain ideas or concepts
  e.g. classify, describe, summarise, clarify, predict, retell
- **Applying** – use information in new situations
  e.g. solve, demonstrate, interpret, respond, carry out, provide, use
- **Analysing** – draw connections amongst ideas
  e.g. compare, contrast, examine, question, differentiate, deconstruct

Higher-order thinking

- **Evaluating** – justify a stand or decision
  e.g. argue, critique, judge, defend, determine, reflect
- **Creating** – produce new or original work
  e.g. design, construct, develop, formulate

Application in teaching

- Bloom's revised taxonomy, particularly the action verbs, can be used as a basis for constructing questions that require different levels of thinking.
- Educators must plan worthwhile questions to deepen and further pupils' understanding, rather than ask them to recall a simple fact (Shirley Clarke Education, 2021a).

Questioning in the classroom

- There has been plentiful research into the types of question asked in the classroom and their impact on learning.
- According to Blosser there are four main types of question used in the classroom (Blosser, 1975):

- **Managerial** – keep the classroom operating
  e.g. Who has finished?
- **Rhetorical** – emphasise a point or reinforce an idea
  e.g. Are you listening?
- **Closed** – check retention or focus thinking
  e.g. What is 4 + 4?
- **Open** – promote discussion or student interaction
  e.g. How do you know?

- Questions that assess knowledge and understanding are often closed and based on recall of facts; however, questions that invoke higher-order thinking (HOT) are often open-ended, promote discussion and require justification.

Are HOT questions actually used?

- According to Hattie, pupil responses to teacher questions average around two or three words (or are less than five seconds long) approximately 70 per cent of the time (Hattie, 2012).
- In Lavender Primary School, feedback from teachers who had analysed their lesson videos indicated that much more time is spent asking closed questions to recall facts or managerial questions about procedures than is spent on those that require higher-order thinking. They also noted that meaningful questions asked by pupils were rare.

Criticisms of Bloom's Taxonomy

It is important to note that Bloom's taxonomy has received its fair share of criticism, such as the following summarised by Berger (2018):

- It does not accurately represent how we learn.
- Learning is not a hierarchy or linear process – it is not possible to perform one of these skills separately from the others.
- Knowledge/remembering is the foundation of learning – it should not be devalued or seen as less important or difficult.
- Emphasis should not be on which process to choose or on moving up the pyramid, but on balance – every part matters.

Putting it into practice

For leaders

- Ensure quality training on questioning is provided for all staff, including new teachers.
- Ask teachers to video one of their lessons and analyse their questioning (managerial, knowledge or higher-order) by making a tally. They could then discuss and reflect on their findings with a colleague.
- Ask teachers to include key questions on the planning for all subject areas.
- Create a questioning environment across the school that encourages children to ask questions.

For teachers

- Make the verbs from the revised taxonomy part of classroom language; model and refer to them on the working wall (see further reading for action verb list).
- Explicitly teach children how to question effectively to develop their techniques and ensure there is time put aside for them to ask and answer their own questions.

- Try a variety of 'no-hands-up' strategies: allow thinking time and partner talk before questioning through think-pair-share.
- Extend questioning and probe children to develop their answers: Why do you think that? How do you know? Can you explain why? Can you give me an example?
- Encourage children to extend others' answers or agree/disagree respectfully.
- Use prompts or encouragers: What would you say if…? Have you compared your idea with…? Can you explain what you mean by…?
- Use a statement and ask them to prove it or say whether it is always, sometimes or never true, and, more importantly, why.
- Use sentence stems or cloze activities to scaffold children's responses.
- Use images, texts or film clips as inspiration for questions (see further reading for more ideas and strategies to develop questioning).

Key quote

'No one can teach, if by teaching we mean the transmission of knowledge from one person to another. The most that can be done is that one person more knowledgeable than another can, by asking him a series of questions, stimulate the other to think, and so cause him to learn for himself.' (Socrates, 5th century BC)

Further reading

- Gilbert, I. (2007), *The Little Book of Thunks*. Carmarthen: Crown House Publishing.

  (For a collection of open questions designed to get children thinking and discussing)

- Revised Bloom's Taxonomy action verbs, www.apu.edu/live_data/files/333/blooms_taxonomy_action_verbs.pdf
  (Action verbs to support with framing questions under the six thinking levels)
- Shirley Clarke Education (2021a) Formative assessment: A summary, www.shirleyclarke-education.org/what-is-formative-assessment
  (For more questioning templates to support teachers with framing questions)

So, we worked to develop an 'effective questioning' approach at Lavender. Children were beginning to get the idea that there wasn't necessarily just a yes or no answer and that learning can involve a deeper level of thinking, as well as collaborative discussion and exploration. These ideas are integral to our Fast Feedback approach, which draws upon children being able to understand what it means to learn. However, they (and we) were right at the beginning of this journey and we found that there were a few things about our learning culture that needed some work!

Something was missing

To find out what the first thing that was missing was, let me take you back to my teaching in the summer of 2011. It was the perfect AFL classroom. The sun streamed through the window and was caught by a crystal from a beaded curtain (the doorway to a magical role-play area). This sent a rainbow across the carpet, where sat 30 learners: little ones with faces lifted in anticipation. Ready to give their thoughts. Waiting for the lolly-stick to be chosen…

Each teacher had a little bit of creative licence with their lolly-stick pots. Some were jam jars covered in colourful paper or stickers, whilst others were more elegant – picked up during a trip to IKEA. Mine was one of the latter. Blue frosted glass and I liked to shake it before I picked. Build the tension a bit (come on, teachers with lolly-stick pots – you know you like to do that too!). The children had had their chance to think for the recommended time (which was one whole minute, but I always struggled to wait that long, especially in an observation) and they'd had a meaningful discussion with their partner.

So, there I was, shaking my sticks, when suddenly something shook me. Ariana, one of the higher achievers, was sitting right at the front where she liked to be, eager to learn, confident, sweet (you know the type: a teacher favourite if we were allowed to have one but we're not). I shook the pot and Ariana shuddered. Yes. She visibly shuddered! 'Ariana, what's wrong? Don't you like the lolly-sticks?'

She looked a little guilty, but she followed the core values always and honesty was one of them, remember. 'Not really, no,' she replied in a little voice.

I addressed the whole class, discarding the no-hands-up policy in a flash. Put your hand up if you like the lolly-sticks. Roughly half the class. Put your hand up if you don't like the lolly-sticks. Roughly half the class. Further questioning revealed that some wanted to be picked more often and some were terrified of being picked. Some wanted to be picked some of the time, but not all of the time. Something was wrong here. Although we'd worked on developing the core value of respect, meaning that children shouldn't be afraid of 'getting something wrong' in front of their classmates, there was still something missing. I delved into the Shirley Clarke book and there it was – a missed chapter!

I devoured that chapter. I Googled Carol Dweck, watched her YouTube videos and read all the bits and pieces I could find about growth mindset (you can do the same by skipping ahead to the fact file on growth mindset in the next chapter). Then I persuaded Matthew to let me do a staff INSET on growth mindset. As I may have mentioned, he is a leader who values innovation and didn't actually need much persuasion. I argued that we had been in such a rush to do the 'visible bits' of formative assessment that the most important part, creating the right culture for it, had been skipped. 'Go for it' I think were his words.

Quick Tip: Don't rush to bring in an initiative without doing all the background reading first (especially this one!).

You may or may not believe in 'no hands up' (or use hands up strategically as Lavender now does) and may or may not use lolly-sticks. Regardless, having the right mindset is crucial to the success of introducing Fast Feedback, so we will explore what it is and why it is so important.

Before we do that, here is a quick summary of some of the key points raised in this chapter:

Chapter Summary

- A behaviour policy that promotes respect between all members of the school community can add to the positive ethos of a school.
- School values should be applied to learning as well as social behaviour.
- Rushing in a strategy (such as no hands up) without creating the right culture can be counterproductive.
- Good questioning leads to deeper thinking and helps to create the right learning culture.

3 It's all in the mind *Developing resilient learners*

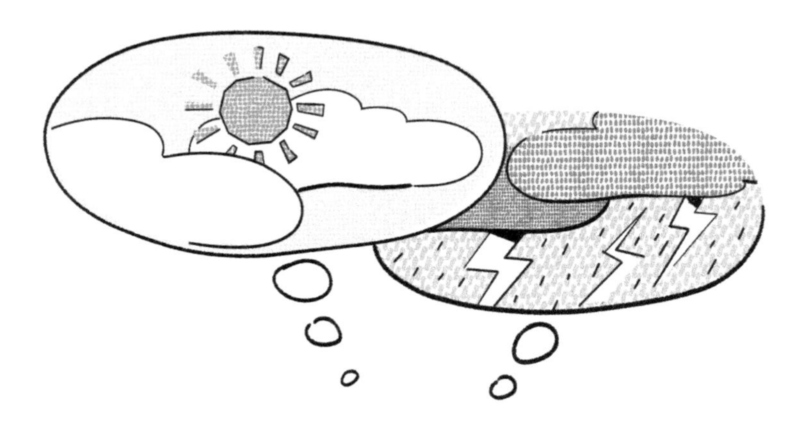

First day at school

It was Jodie's first day at Lavender Primary School. She sat in the middle of the group because at the front she would be too noticeable and at the back she might seem disinterested. It was a strategic decision and she felt pleased with herself and ready to learn. But there were soon to be anxiety and tears. The tears came first.

The 2011 September staff INSET started with an introduction from Matthew. He talked about the school vision, and about policy and expectations. He also put forward some fascinating viewpoints of how we learn, sharing with us Matthew Syed's book *Bounce* (2011). Jodie was excited; it was looking to be an interesting and informative morning (… and yes, she's a grown-up).

Then it was Chris's turn. At that time, we were embedding our core values and 'determination' was a real favourite, influenced heavily by the 2012 Olympics. Chris, our deputy at the time, really wanted us to see that value in action so, before some inspiring maths training on the power of 5, he showed us a video. It was a video of Derek Redmond in the 1992 Olympics, set to the music of *You Raise Me Up* by Josh Groban. You may have seen it. You may have cried. If you haven't, search 'Derek Redmond. Never Give Up' (there are a number of versions online). Have the tissues ready. Most Lavender staff shed tears, as did Jodie – on her very first day.

Then came anxiety.

Getting the message across

I was next on the INSET agenda, and I had a very important message that I wanted to share: 'There's something wrong with how we're using lolly-sticks!' (A child had shuddered when I shook the lolly-stick pot, for goodness' sake.)

Quick Question: Are some of your children genuinely worried about answering questions in front of the class? Or just in small groups, or one to one for that matter?

After that reaction to my pot-shaking, and the subsequent research, I realised that we had to develop more resilience in our children. We needed to nurture a 'growth mindset' at Lavender, and my job that morning was to get buy-in from the staff. They needed to understand what had happened. Here is what I did.

Whilst showing the 'Aims' slide, I highlighted that classroom culture, creative curriculum, pupil choice, pupil-generated success criteria, dialogic talk and self- and peer-evaluation were all elements, within the 'Aims', that we would be exploring during the session.

Then I held up the lolly-stick pot.

'I really want the contributions to be fair,' I explained, with the sincerest voice I could muster. 'But I know that some of you will have lots to say about certain topics, and others might not get a chance to give their thoughts… [cue the concerned face]… even though they'd like to. So, to ensure that *everyone* has the opportunity to speak, I've written all your names on lolly-sticks and I'll pick one at key discussion points throughout the training.'

Pause. Deathly silence.

Shake the sticks.

'And if I pick your name, perhaps you could stand up, or come to the front if you'd prefer, and just give your thoughts about whatever topic we're looking at or discussing at that moment.'

Deathly silence.

'That way [relentless], everyone gets a chance to speak. I do hope that's OK…' This was a statement, not a question. There was no room for negotiation.

Mumbling and murmuring.

'Actually, on your tables there is a little pile of printed thought bubbles. Please can you write on one exactly how you feel about what I just said – about having your names on lolly-sticks to be picked. Be honest. You don't have to share what you write.'

But they did share. Boy did they share. Some of the comments can't possibly be repeated here; one was in a similar vein to the comments made by children before Matthew's new behaviour policy. Four-lettered words aside, there were thoughts such as, 'Oh God, that's scary', 'I don't know anything about dialogic talk!' and 'Why would she do this to us?' There was even a 'bring it on!'

I recently spoke with Jodie about her experience back then – her first day at Lavender. She told me, 'My stomach was churning. It was my first day and I was terrified of looking like an idiot the first time that people heard me speak. I totally understood how some children must feel!'

> **Quick Question: Are some of the staff at your school genuinely worried about asking or answering questions in front of their peers? Are you?**

I have gone on to do this cruel lolly-stick exercise as a training opener in many schools (in the UK and abroad), at academy trust and governor conferences, at local authority training and (my favourite) with fourth-year BEd primary students. It is always the same: mostly horrified negativity with the odd splash of 'bring it on'. Over the years I progressed from little paper thought bubbles to cool techy feedback, using participant mobile phones to create anonymous wordles of their thoughts. See Figure 2.1 for a wordle done a few years back with the BEd students. I so love their honesty!

Once I'd terrified most Lavender staff, we went on to consider how to develop resilient, confident learners. Using ideas from the research of Carol Dweck and Shirley Clarke, we explored thoughts around intelligence and the promotion of growth mindset. These ideas are set out in this chapter's fact file on mindset and resilience.

Figure 2.1 *Getting the message about growth mindset across – the emotions some adults might experience when the lolly-sticks are used on them!*

FACT FILE: MINDSET AND RESILIENCE

What

Mindset is a set of beliefs that affect how you think, feel and behave and can be applied to learning and intelligence. Resilience, the capacity to recover quickly from difficulties and adapt when things go wrong, can be the determining factor in success.

Why mindset and resilience are important to Fast Feedback

If children are to take control of their own learning and become self-regulatory learners, then it is crucial that they have the right mindset. Fear of appearing 'stupid' will cause problems when they are expected to honestly evaluate and mark their own work, or carry out cooperative reviews with a peer (key elements of Fast Feedback). A lack of resilience will lead to a lack of drive and determination to make improvements to their work after reflection and feedback.

Key people

Carol Dweck

Carol Dweck is a psychologist and leading researcher into the fields of personality, social and developmental psychology. Her book *Mindset* was written in 2006.

Key messages

- In her early research into motivation and how people cope with failure, Dweck sought to understand the power of mindsets and their impact on achievement.

- She observed that when presented with a problem that was too difficult, *successful* students didn't see it as failing at all, but as learning: they thrived on the challenge and persevered until the end.
- Dweck proposed that it is not ability but beliefs about ability that can have an impact on success.
- It is the view that we adopt for ourselves, conscious and unconscious thoughts that guide our behaviour and propel or prevent us from fulfilling our potential.

Dweck established two mindsets that affect why we succeed and why we don't:

The fixed mindset *The tyranny of now*	**The growth mindset** *The power of yet*
• Intelligence is static and qualities are set in stone.	• Intelligence and qualities can be cultivated.
• It's about succeeding and being perfect right now.	• It's about potential to succeed in the future.
• Challenges are feared.	• Challenges are embraced.
• Obstacles are avoided.	• Obstacles are dealt with and overcome.
• Risks are not taken.	• Risks are taken.
• Effort is devalued.	• Effort is the path to mastery.
• Criticism is ignored.	• Criticism is welcomed and learned from.
• Others are a threat.	• Others are an inspiration.
• Failure defines you.	• Failure can be learned from.
• Desire to prove yourself and seek confirmation of your intelligence, personality or character.	• Desire to reach higher levels of achievement and seek to grow your true potential through application and experience.

(Dweck, 2017)

Putting it into practice

For leaders

- Ask staff to generate and share feedback phrases that promote a growth mindset.
- Ensure growth mindset training is given to all new staff.
- Have a school display on mindset – you could get the children to design it!
- Refer to mindset regularly in assemblies or whole-school events.
- Hold an information event or training for parents and governors on mindset.

For teachers

- Plan and teach regular/termly growth mindset lessons to the children, rather than just a one-off lesson at the beginning of the year.
- Refer to mindset regularly in lessons and at other points during the school day.
- Address stereotypes, for example, by ordering different professionals according to their 'intelligence'.
- Share stories that involve characters overcoming challenges.
- Have a classroom display on mindset: mind-map positive phrases with the children, refer to it and add to it (rather than letting it become wallpaper!).
- Praise the process, their strategies and perseverance and reward effort over achievement.
- Use language such as 'yet' and 'not yet' to encourage persistence.

- Encourage pupils to share and compare strategies for seeing a tricky problem through to the end.
- Be aware and understanding of pupils who may find growth mindset a challenge and need extra support, particularly in creative subjects like art.

Key quote

'A person's true potential is unknown (and unknowable)... it's impossible to foresee what can be accomplished with years of passion, toil, and training.' (Dweck, 2006, p. 7)

Further reading

- Dweck, C. S. (2014), The power of believing that you can improve, www.ted.com/talks/carol_dweck_the_power_of_believing_that_you_can_improve

  (A short introduction into the power of growth mindset; it describes two ways to think about a problem that's slightly too hard for you to solve)
- Dweck, C. S. (2017), *Mindset: Changing the way you think to fulfil your potential* (updated edition). New York: Random House.

  (This updated version includes a section on false growth mindsets and changing mindsets)
- Mindset Works (2017), The impact of a growth mindset, www.mindsetworks.com/Science/Impact

  (For further research and evidence into the impact of growth mindset)

Creating the mindset

As well as frightening participants during my mindset training sessions, I've also encouraged them to explore how to use the right words and phrases to promote perseverance, effort and determination. A friend and colleague once highlighted for me how she unwittingly used damaging phrases with her son for years. She told Fred he was clever. She told Fred he was a quick learner. She called him intelligent and praised him for how easy he found things. Fred's mindset by the time he got to secondary school was, 'If I don't learn something quickly, I can't be clever. If I don't find things easy, I'm not intelligent.' When things were a little more challenging for Fred in secondary school, or took time and effort, he would give up. The fear of failure and the fear of not looking 'intelligent' meant that he wouldn't even try. Don't worry, it all worked out OK in the end but only after a mindset reset.

> **Quick Question: Do your staff use phrases that promote a 'growth' or 'fixed' mindset?**

Without the right mindset, children marking their own work might not always go to plan. Lavender children had already started self-assessing their writing against the toolkit (as you may remember from discussion around our Big Writing expectations in Chapter 1), but we had noticed that this wasn't always what we'd expect to see. Before embedding the right culture, many children had just done the ticks as an exercise, thinking they'd got it right or, as was often the case, because they didn't want to look 'stupid'.

We found the same thing happening in maths, where children were also encouraged to self-assess. Oh and by the way, the marking policy nonsense extended to other subjects too. Indeed, when trawling through hard drives full of policy madness for this book, I came across an early maths marking and feedback policy. The focus on pen colour is ridiculous. We really did have a thing about it back then. Here are a few little snippets for fun:

> *The children self-assess their work at the end of the lesson by marking against their title with a tick or a dot, in* pencil…
>
> *Work is to be marked daily in* GREEN *pen.*
>
> *Children will respond to any marking before starting new tasks – this could be with a comment, smiley face, 'thank you', etc. or initials. This will be in* RED *pen.*
>
> *The children will complete their task in* RED *pen.*

And yes, there were pencil ticks when there should have been dots. So, without doubt, promoting the right mindset is crucial if you are going to expect children to mark their own work, to critique one another and themselves, to push themselves and to become self-regulatory learners. They need to be honest about where they are in their learning, but fear of appearing 'unintelligent' will hinder them when judging their progress against the toolkit and self-assessing their maths work. They also need to be resilient and determined to make more progress. Reworking a piece of text, developing a piece of artwork or restarting a maths problem requires effort and persistence. With a fixed mindset that just says, 'you're as good as you're gonna get', that reworking is not going to happen – well, not in any meaningful way – and many children would have no determination or drive to improve things.

Carol Dweck's advice on praising effort and resilience seems so obvious to us all now.

It became policy then, back in 2011, that teachers should deliver well-planned and timetabled lessons on the concept of intelligence, growth mindset and determination. All staff were expected to refer to growth mindset whenever an opportunity arose, praising those children who were showing it. The word 'can't' became a dirty word until we realised that we could add 'yet' very successfully. We also made a small, but significant, change to the wording of the toolkit from 'I can' to 'I am learning to', which helped to promote children's honesty about their learning and to see learning as a journey.

All teachers also had to have a dedicated display in their classrooms filled with encouraging phrases around positivity and determination. Wherever possible, these were created with the children. The colour printing and laminating costs hit the roof and our own contribution to damaging the environment increased tenfold.

We can do it!

So, the school looked fabulous! I'd walk into a classroom and there would be the Growth Mindset Tree with leaves of encouragement: try again, work hard, don't be scared, don't laugh at your friend, if at first you don't succeed (the old favourite made an appearance or two), never give up. We had trees, we had ladders and there was even a Determination Dog with, I think, Positive Comment Fleas (all right, probably not, but you get the idea of how creative things were). Tracy's 'Ms I Can' and 'Ms I Can't' puppets, which made regular visits to the nursery and Reception classes, were simply adorable.

Another creative teacher worked extra hard to make growth mindset fun for her kids. She developed, with them, a little chant, which went like this:

> *'We can do it! We can do it!*
>
> *Can we do it? Yes we can!'*
>
> How cute is that? (And they were Year 1 – so 'extra' cute.) They'd march around the playground during PE warm up...
>
> *'We can do it, we can do it...'*
>
> They'd sit on the carpet after input and, just before going off to their tables...
>
> *'We can do it, we can do it...'*

They even made the chant part of their sharing assembly. Oh boy the parents loved it...

'We can do it, we can do it. Can we do it? Yes we can!'

BUT

THEY

COULDN'T.

Well, to be fair, lots of them could do it, but quite a few of them couldn't. There were those children who would chant until their hearts were bursting with determination, but they were still struggling to grasp certain concepts or achieve their targets.

Don't get me wrong. Developing that determination and resilience was without doubt one of the key reasons that we could go ahead with the Fast Feedback approach. As already highlighted, it makes a significant difference to children's attitudes towards learning. Lavender pupils learned that success required effort and that pushing themselves to achieve more was a good thing. They knew that it was OK to answer a question and be wrong (this was particularly empowering for those higher-achieving children who find it so hard to 'get something wrong'). They were on the right path. The attitude was there. However, if we wanted our children to become independent, self-regulatory learners who didn't need written comments on their work to understand where they were, then attitude alone wasn't enough.

We needed them to learn how to be good learners. We needed our children to 'know about' and *own* their learning. We'll look at how we approached that in the next chapter, but first a quick recap of some key messages in this one:

Chapter Summary

- Staff training that is well thought-out and designed to make your message clear will promote buy-in.
- The ideas around growth mindset should be shared with the whole school community, not just class teachers.
- Developing the right mindset will promote children's attitudes towards learning.
- Classroom displays and motivational quotes alone won't guarantee a change in mindset across the school.

4 Lavender learns to learn *Developing children as effective learners*

Pupil choice and pupil voice

Ownership of learning had been a theme at Lavender since 2009. During that year, Matthew had organised for me and a colleague to see a curriculum presentation from another school and we were truly dazzled. This was innovation. For almost two years, Bowes Primary School had fully engaged their children through their 'Learning Journey' approach, which allowed each class to choose their own topic. We walked around the school and witnessed fabulously dressed doorways, each depicting that class's journey. Teacher creativity was at an all-time high and children's enthusiasm for learning was unfettered. We loved it. After assessing where we were with curriculum engagement, through pupil questionnaires, we followed suit and introduced the Lavender Creative Curriculum. It was fairly easy to develop lessons around the pupil-chosen cross-curricular theme and link them with the required knowledge and skills to be learned. For instance, those values characters that appeared in Chapter 2 were the result of my Year 2 class choosing 'The Mr Men' as a topic and my need to deliver a PSHE curriculum.

OK, I said it was 'fairly easy' to deliver this curriculum but, as teacher workload is a dominant theme of this book, I will be honest: it really wasn't that easy. My Year 1 class choosing 'Ballet' as their topic title one term almost sent me pirouetting into the sunset. The struggle, for our teachers, was coming up with creative lesson ideas to cover all the required skills and knowledge. This became obvious to me as a leader, eventually. A few years into our creative curriculum, I was astonished that Class X had chosen 'Robots'... again!

'Wow, what a coincidence!'

Not only that, but on more than one occasion all three classes in a year group would choose the very same topic.

'How does that happen!?'

Yes, you guessed it, the poor teachers were trying to reduce their workload. Remember, we were marking then as well. Teacher creativity was certainly at an all-time high: they were being highly creative in managing their children's choices and, consequently, their work–life balance.

Quick Tip: No matter how exciting an initiative, always consider it in terms of workload, and try to maintain a balance.

So, we reduced the amount of pupil choice topics that were required but we still encouraged 'pupil voice', where children had a say in *how* they studied a theme or topic. This approach continues to work perfectly well alongside a more 'knowledge-rich' and individual subject-focused curriculum. By the way, the ongoing discussions about knowledge vs skills is a fascinating one and I'm looking forward to an enjoyable read of Guy Claxton's book *The Future of Teaching and the Myths That Hold It Back* (2021). I'm not going into a big debate about statutory curriculum requirements or Department for Education recommendations here ('thank goodness,' I hear you say) but suffice it to say that Lavender children's ownership over how they were learning not only engaged and motivated them, but also put them in a good place when we asked them to mark their own work. It made more sense to them.

Quick Question: Do children in your school have a voice in what, or how, they learn?

As mentioned previously, self-marking was introduced at Lavender some years before we implemented Fast Feedback as an approach. Children were already self-assessing their compositions by ticking the toolkit before the teacher marked the work, and we'd also given them some ownership of their maths learning.

Self-challenge

After the maths teaching input, the children would decide themselves on the challenge they needed by choosing from three different levels of worksheets. The tasks were labelled Tricky, Trickier and Trickiest (the idea of a class teacher at the time, to embed the idea that there would always be some element of challenge and effort in learning). The answers were there on the tables for children to check after solving a few problems. If some were wrong, they would unpick the steps they had gone through to identify the error or misconception. This analysis of their own outcomes enabled our learners to change their approach to work on a solution. If they couldn't work out where they'd gone wrong, the teacher would step in to guide or reteach through a face-to-face conference (you'll be hearing much more about 'conferences' and how they are managed in Ivy Learning Trust schools in coming chapters, as they are a mainstay of the Fast Feedback approach).

Quick Tip: If you are a marking school, try putting maths answers on the table so that children can self-mark. It's a gentle introduction to Fast Feedback. But please make sure they have the right mindset first!

When children make comments such as 'I'm going to do the Trickier as this is too easy' or 'I can't work out where I went wrong, please can you help?', you know the mindset is right and you're onto something. Some years later, Lavender purchased a Singapore Maths scheme, where the reflective approach and decisions around which strategy to use to solve a problem fitted perfectly with challenge and ownership.

Without doubt, the work done around growth mindset and the value of honesty helped us with our 'ownership of learning' approach. The children were confident enough to say, 'This is hard', 'I don't get it' and 'I think I need to do it again'. But as I highlighted before, positive, honest attitude and perseverance doesn't guarantee successful learning. Indeed, as Carol Dweck pointed out in her 2016 interview with Christine Gross-Loh for *The Atlantic*: 'Students need to know that if they're stuck, they don't need just effort. You don't want them redoubling their efforts with the same ineffective strategies.' (Dweck, 2016)

Cute chanting, praise for effort and resilience, and a school full of empowering quotes (no matter how ingeniously displayed) just weren't enough. The ownership of learning had begun but our children needed other skills to truly own, and take forward, their learning.

The skills of learning

We turned to the work of Guy Claxton and his great ideas in *Building Learning Power* (Claxton, 2002). There we finally discovered the skills of learning that we needed our children to employ and got to work implementing 'learning to learn'. This meant that our children would be helped to understand that effective learning means drawing upon a range of skills and behaviours, such as questioning, reasoning, reflecting, working alone or with others, and being resourceful, to mention just a few. We needed them to learn how to learn and to begin to understand themselves as learners – to become self-regulatory, lifelong learners.

Some years later, in 2018, the Education Endowment Foundation published its excellent guide on metacognition and self-regulation (EEF, 2018), which complemented and, along with Guy Claxton's updated Teacher's Palette (BLP, 2018a), extended the work we were doing on meta-learning.

Claxton's approach is well known now, but as this is such a key component of Fast Feedback, it is worth looking in more detail at his and the EEF's ideas in this chapter's fact file on effective learners.

FACT FILE: EFFECTIVE LEARNERS

What

Metacognition and self-regulation approaches support pupils to know the skills of learning and think about their own learning more explicitly in order to become the most effective learners. Metacognition is the way in which learners monitor, purposefully direct and review their learning, often linked to 'meta-learning' or 'learning to learn'. Self-regulation is the extent to which learners are aware of their strengths

and weaknesses and the strategies they use to motivate themselves and improve their learning (EEF, 2018).

Why metacognition is important to Fast Feedback

Our approach hands over responsibility for marking to the child, with the teacher as guide and facilitator. Learning how to learn helps children to reflect on their own learning, mark their own work, evaluate their successes and areas for development and set themselves follow-up tasks. Effective learners will begin to recognise the skills they have used, the strategies they need to employ and the learning behaviours that they need to develop.

Key people

Guy Claxton

Guy Claxton is a cognitive scientist and writer of books on psychology and education. He is the pioneer of the 'learning power' concept, which expands children's capacity for learning in the classroom. His practical book for teachers *Building Learning Power* was written in 2002.

Key messages

Building Learning Power (BLP) (Claxton, 2018)

- Learning power regards ability and inclination to learn.
- BLP is an approach for helping young people become better, lifelong learners.

- Effective learners need to be good at: observing, reading, critiquing, experimenting, imagining, reasoning, imitating and discussing.
- They must also be good at reflecting (metacognition) and be perceptive, honest observers and critics of their own performance.
- Developing this self-awareness is not easy – it requires skilful coaching and a learning-friendly culture to build better learners.

The Learning Power Equation (BLP, 2018b)

Learning-friendly classroom cultures: promote curious, confident, independent learners	+	A language for learning: make the *how* of learning explicit by talking the language of learning	=	A powerful learning character: learners for life

The Teachers' Palette (BLP, 2018a)

- Teachers must employ a palette of techniques to create a learning-friendly culture.
- The pupil's role changes from receptive to active; the teacher's role from delivering content to constructing situations that uncover the learning.
- The palette has been updated to include the types of actions teachers need to take to ensure learning behaviours are habituated.

The Revised Teachers' Palette (BLP, 2018a)

- **Relating** – *modelling, coaching, devolving* (making learning a shared responsibility).
- **Talking** – *exploring process, language of learning, nudging progress* (making learning the object of conversation).
- **Constructing** – *activities: challenging, dual-focused, reflective* (making learning the object of learning).
- **Celebrating** – *growing habits, redefining failure, displaying values* (making learning the object of attention).

The Supple Learning Mind (New Domains of Learning):

This has been updated since the original Four Domains of Learning (or 4 Rs) to acknowledge the complexities of learning power (BLP, 2018a):

- The emotional (feeling) domain – with capacities that build resilient learners.
- The cognitive (thinking) domain – with capacities that build resourceful learners.
- The social (relating) domain – with capacities that build reciprocal learners.
- The strategic (managing) domain – with capacities that build reflective (metacognitive) learners.

Self-regulated learning

According to the EEF (2018), there are three essential components to self-regulated learning:

- **Cognition** – the mental process involved in knowing, understanding and learning.
- **Metacognition** – the ways learners monitor and purposefully direct their learning (learning to learn).
- **Motivation** – a willingness to engage metacognitive and cognitive skills.

The EEF's Teaching and Learning Toolkit (EEF, 2018), based on a summary of international evidence on teaching five- to 16-year-olds, also supports the importance of metacognition and self-regulation on outcomes.

These are the findings outlined in their guidance report:

- Metacognition and self-regulation are high impact for very low cost.
- Developing pupils' metacognitive knowledge of how they learn and their knowledge of themselves as learners improves pupils' outcomes.
- Metacognition and self-regulation are hard to teach, but are powerful levers for boosting learning.
- Teachers must give pupils a repertoire of strategies to choose from and the skills to select the most suitable strategy for each learning task.
- As a result of the findings, the EEF proposed seven key recommendations (see EEF, 2018, in further reading).

Putting it into practice

For leaders

- Provide opportunities for staff to know themselves as learners and support them to develop knowledge of the approaches using the EEF recommendations.

- Ask teachers to audit their own teaching against the EEF recommendations.
- Share teacher experiences and strategies to implement it effectively into daily practice.
- Have whole-school displays and assemblies that promote effective learning strategies.
- Share effective learning strategies with parents and carers through presentations or workshops.

For teachers

- Provide a variety of lessons.
- Hold discussions with your class about how they learn and identify meta-learning vocabulary.
- Have a 'how we learn' display in the classroom and refer to it during lessons.
- Ensure children are explicitly taught how to learn, focusing on each domain of the Supple Learning Mind (BLP, 2018a), and that this is reviewed/recapped regularly.
- Ask children to complete a questionnaire to identify their learning behaviours.
- Ask children to carry out a task with/without distractions and ask them to consider the difference in terms of impact on learning.
- Make sure the learning intention is specific and focuses on metacognition, for example, 'I am learning to recognise my own learning strengths.'
- Work with a small group on a challenging task and follow this with a discussion around how they succeeded or what they would do differently next time.
- Use 'split-screen teaching' to encourage metacognitive talk across the curriculum.

- Ask meta-learning questions, such as: What helps you to learn? What stops you from learning? What does a successful learner do/look like?
- Support pupils to use a range of strategies for planning, monitoring and evaluating their own learning.
- In maths, encourage children to attempt one or two questions, mark their work and consider where they are going wrong and how to correct it before continuing.
- Coach pupils to reflect and think more deeply about their learning (see Jim Smith's *The Lazy Teacher's Handbook* (2017) for activities).
- Use a variety of strategies for AFL, for example, thumbs up/down, traffic lighting, tick or dot in books.
- Facilitate opportunities for peer learning and talk-partner work to enable children to learn from each other.

Key quote

'Knowledge is what you know, or know how to do. Learning is a change in what you know, or can do. And learning power is a change in the way you go about learning.' (Claxton, 2018, p. 529)

Further reading

- Building Learning Power (BLP) (2018a), Creating learning friendly classroom cultures, www.buildinglearningpower.com/2018/05/creating-metacognitive-classroom-cultures *(For more information about the new Teacher's Palette and how to approach Building Learning Power in the classroom)*
- Claxton, G. (2018), *The Learning Power Approach: Teaching learners to teach themselves.* Carmarthen: Crown House Publishing.

(For the principles of a way of teaching that aims to strengthen students' learning and develop their independence)

- Education Endowment Foundation (EEF) (2020), Metacognition and self-regulated learning: Learning guidance report: Seven recommendations for teaching self-regulated learning & metacognition,

  https://educationendowmentfoundation.org.uk/tools/guidance-reports/metacognition-and-self-regulated-learning

  (For the full summary of practical, evidence-based recommendations to support teachers to develop metacognitive knowledge in their pupils)
- Smith, J. (2017), *The Lazy Teacher's Handbook: How your students learn more when you teach less* (updated edition). Carmarthen: Crown House Publishing

  (For more tips and activities that take the emphasis away from teaching and put it onto learning)

A policy for learning

The Lavender teaching and learning policy of 2012–2013 was somewhat comprehensive. It mentioned values, wellbeing, formative assessment, assessment for learning, self-assessment, creative curriculum, challenge, questioning, homework, PE kit and countless other things. Four full pages of Comic Sans 11pt – the holy grail of school typefaces. This policy even mentioned the other policies and documents that should be read in conjunction with it! Every class teacher had a special purple folder (a big one) to keep all their policies in, but goodness only knows how they found time to read them all. Crucially, any policy change didn't happen without some CPD first (that was in the policy too). Our bullet point on growth mindset in 2012 became one on growth mindset and learning to learn in 2013.

- *We aim to create and maintain a 'Growth Mindset' and Learning 2 Learn culture where all children feel able to achieve and can take responsibility for their own learning.*

Did that mean that we achieved it straight away? No. It took time and, like every other initiative, it meant revisits. Actually, that's a really important point – and I'm talking to leaders here – if you introduce an approach, it could be very easy, once the excitement has died down, to forget that you now have a new member of staff or two who might not know about good questioning, growth mindset, think, pair, share, and so on. I'm not saying that we ever did forget that... OK, we did, but we quickly learned that we needed to have a clear set of induction training for all new teachers and support staff.

Quick Tip: When new staff join your school, ensure that they are given induction training around the pedagogy *behind* your policies and expectations.

I think it's important to point out here that I'm not a pedagogy specialist, haven't studied neuroscience (yet) and most certainly am not an education theory expert so, apart from the fact file above, I won't go into detail about the EEF papers and Building Learning Power but (along with the updates) they are recommended reading. In the meantime, I'll share with you a snapshot of how certain learning to learn skills helped us to move towards no marking and our successful Fast Feedback approach.

What is a good learner?

Being a class teacher was my opportunity to be creative. I loved planning lessons, creating class sharing assemblies and producing classroom displays. Becoming a senior leader gave me less of those opportunities so I took them where I could, and staff INSET became one of my favourite things to do. Let's face it, we've talked about engaging children but are staff meetings always as engaging as they should be, or is it more often a case of 'death by PowerPoint'? One of my favourite go-to resources for inspiration was Jim Smith's *The Lazy Teacher's Handbook* (Smith, 2017). I'd been to one of his presentations and was sold. The ideas are fun and give great results and I've used many of them in staff training sessions. For our very first learning to learn staff meeting, I used his 'Arrest me' idea. To encourage people to start thinking about how we learn, I announced:

> *YOU'VE BEEN ARRESTED AND CHARGED WITH BEING A GOOD LEARNER. LIST THE EVIDENCE THAT WOULD BE USED AGAINST YOU.*

The gathered information and ensuing discussion led nicely on to, what was then, Guy Claxton's 4 Rs.

> Quick Tip: Resources designed for teachers to use with pupils can be adapted for adults to make CPD more interactive and fun.

Claxton's description of resilience includes discussion on giving it a go, liking a challenge and not being frightened of finding things difficult or getting things wrong. Our children were already well practised in showing the core value of 'determination' and knew that perseverance was important. 'Never give up' was one of the repetitive lines of the Lavender song and they knew that learning involved effort. The work on growth mindset had put us in a good place. So too had our approach on 'challenge'.

Remember Vygotsky's 'zone of proximal development' (ZPD, 1962) from uni? If you haven't revisited it since, it's worth doing so; there are plenty of straightforward guides to be found online. Some fabulous maths training we'd received from our then maths lead, Corrine, a year or so before introducing learning to learn, had us planning with ZPD in mind and we encouraged teachers to extend this way of thinking to all subjects. Having the right challenge through planning based on formative assessment and maintaining an element of pupil voice helped children to become absorbed in their learning, but 'managing distractions' as an aspect of resilience was a new one for us to explore.

How on earth do you focus on your Big Writing when the teacher is playing Beethoven's 5th at volume (as mentioned in Chapter 1)? As a matter of fact, and I'm sure you know this already, for some people that is exactly what they need. What is key are the discussions that encourage learners to consider and share what helps them to focus and what doesn't. By the way, when I say 'learners' here, naturally I mean the adults as well as the children.

Sharing learning behaviours

Although we didn't do Claxton's Teacher Palette (Claxton, 2002) as a staff INSET until a while after introducing learning to learn, it was stressed that adults, as lifelong learners, must also share their learning behaviours. This was a natural progression from our modelled writing inputs, where teachers would talk through their thoughts on composition, word choice, punctuation and so on (referring to the toolkit, obviously). Oh dear. I feel obliged to admit something here: I never shared with my children that a group phonics lesson going on at the back of a small classroom, during my teaching input, was very, very distracting. L – OU – D (never learned to 'manage' that one).

Quick Question: Do adults at your school share what helps them to learn with their children? Do they speak as learners?

A few paragraphs back, I highlighted the importance of sharing the pedagogy behind policy change with new staff. I also mentioned that change can't happen overnight. Nothing brought that home to me like the voice of the children. In the autumn of 2015, two years after we started 'learning to learn' and a year before implementing Fast Feedback across the school, I set a pupil questionnaire. It asked about homework, values, feeling safe and so on. Some of the responses were encouraging and, I will admit, had the leadership team puffing up with pride. For example:

'Do you enjoy learning?' Pretty much a yes across the whole school.

'What does your teacher do to make sure your work isn't too easy?' Responses covered being able to choose their own level of maths tasks, being given follow-up tasks, being encouraged to challenge themselves and being given a purple pen challenge. (Yep – more ink colour. It won't go away – even when we get to the details of Fast Feedback.)

However, the answers to one key question quickly deflated us and sent us hurtling back to the drawing board.

'Do you know what to do to be a good learner?' Most of the answers that came back, from Year 1 all the way to Year 6, included reference to 'determination and growth mindset', 'follow the values', 'listen to the teacher' and (I kid you not) 'sit nicely'.

Well, this book promised honesty. We'd failed to get a message across, or maybe things had slipped. Probably a bit of both. In truth, looking back at how much we were laying on teachers at that time – a mass of pedagogies and policies being changed, introduced, or promoted (including still getting our heads around the 2014 curriculum) – it's hardly surprising that something had to give.

Oh dear. I've just remembered that we'd also just introduced 'Drafting and Crafting' exhibitions. After an inspiring presentation and a visit to School 21 in East London, Matthew had given the go-ahead for staff training. If you haven't watched EL Education's video 'Austin's Butterfly' (2012) then do so! It's a few years old but still a charming and wonderful lesson on reflection, resilience, peer feedback and, I guess, perfection. However, although our exhibitions were truly 'fabulous' (and ended up being called that), they became just a vehicle for showing off children's work. This is fine, but the pedagogy around drafting work across the curriculum was never embedded at the time. I guess it was enough that our poor staff had to draw upon every ounce of energy possible to produce mini art galleries, after a long day in class, and then stay late to have smiley chats with parents (then, of course, go home to catch up on marking!).

TOO
MUCH
AT
ONCE.

Undoubtedly, there are lessons to be learned here on implementing new initiatives, and this serves as another reminder of the tip in the last chapter – approach every initiative with workload in mind. We will consider this again when we look at theory and practice around change. Workload will affect how well you can embed an initiative and, weirdly, even bringing in a strategy to reduce workload can cause workload and anxiety. More on that later.

Back to the questionnaire on being a good learner now, because (desperately trying to save face here) there were some responses from Year 5 that were far more encouraging, such as: 'manage distractions', 'use resources', 'use the working wall' and 'ask questions'. So, what had these teachers done to embed this? Simple! They'd created fabulous lesson plans for all aspects of becoming a good learner. As a leader, you might want to insist on that. You can provide the lesson plans or let teachers do their own. As a teacher, you'll want some ideas I'm sure, so here are a few tips taken from Sarah's lesson plans (also available in the fact file on effective learners).

- Hold discussions with your class about how they learn and identify meta-learning vocabulary.
- Have a 'how we learn' display in the classroom and refer to it during lessons.
- Ask children to complete a questionnaire to identify their learning behaviours.
- Ask children to carry out a task with and then without distractions and ask them to consider the difference in terms of impact on learning.

- Make sure the learning intention is specific and focuses on metacognition, e.g. I am learning to recognise my own learning strengths.
- Work with a small group on a challenging task and follow up with a discussion around how they succeeded or what they would do differently next time.

In all fairness to ourselves, most Lavender children were using their learning muscles quite well. The problem was that the meta-learning one hadn't been worked on enough, and so we held supplemental staff training sessions and produced whole-school displays to promote it. See Figure 4.1 for a couple of examples from a selection created during a staff INSET on 'how to create effective and interactive displays'. Our school council judged them and awarded a prize to the best. It was lovely.

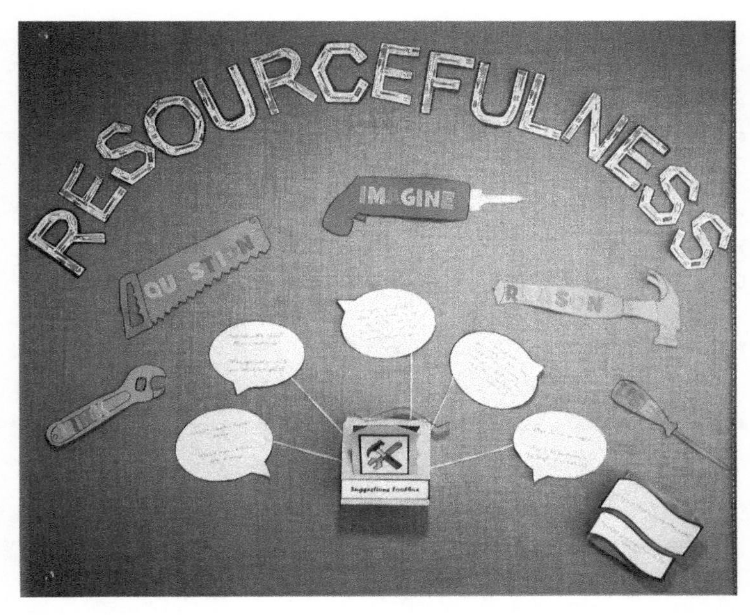

Figure 4.1 *School displays don't have to become wallpaper. Those that are eye-catching and interactive will serve as a teaching tool.*

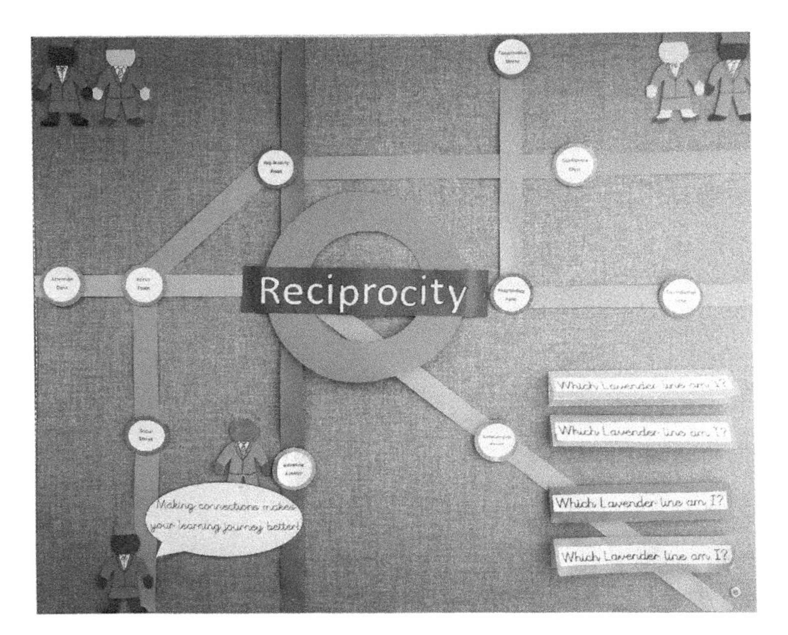

Figure 4.1 *(continued)*

Quick Tip: Don't let learning displays become 'wallpaper' or just words. Children may spout the language of learning (even the hard ones to say like 'reciprocity') but it doesn't mean that the depth of understanding is there.

You must embed ideas that you know are important, and this was very important to us. The EEF pointed out some years later:

> *Developing pupils' metacognitive knowledge of how they learn – their knowledge of themselves as a learner, of strategies, and of tasks – is an effective way of improving pupil outcomes.* (EEF, 2020, Recommendation 1)

We all want to improve outcomes, right? Now, imagine being able to get inside your children's heads to understand exactly what they think about their learning. Well, with Fast Feedback you can. Within our no-marking approach, children often complete a reflection piece after the lesson task and, when children mark their own work and reflect on their learning and progress, you really can *get inside their heads*.

Quick Tip: Reflections don't always have to be written – verbal reflections, shared with a teacher or spoken into a recorder, have a place too.

The children focus on the learning that has just taken place and make comments on how they approached the activity and how they feel they got on. Not only does this help to develop meta-learning, but it also supports the teacher with formative assessment, planning and the identification of key learning points and concepts to cover during the next pupil–teacher conference.

So, without the skills of learning and the right mindset needed for children to do honest self-evaluations and reflections, teachers are disadvantaged when assessing and planning for their classes. For Fast Feedback to work best, it is essential that children are given opportunities to evaluate the work they have completed and to consider themselves as learners. But this doesn't have to be done alone. In true learning to learn style, the approach also draws upon working with others.

Partner work

Partner work has long been an embedded feature at Lavender. For instance, our 'reading buddy' scheme, where older children help younger ones to read, was initiated by Natalie, our then English lead, back in 2012. The Year 6 children had to write an application letter, have an interview and then go through a series of training before being let loose on the little ones.

The EEF Teaching and Learning Toolkit has been updated (EEF, 2018) but still highlights the low-cost positive impact of cross-age tutoring. In 2012, Lavender and a local secondary school carried out a Pupil Premium project that had Year 8 pupils reading with Year 4 children. The following quote from a Year 8 pupil implies the impact of such a project on the growth of metacognitive awareness: 'I have gained knowledge by understanding children's minds.'

Talk partner work was also an essential ingredient of what we considered good classroom practice, and we'd refined the system so that partners were changed regularly. Those teachers who were really organised had fancy, colourful sticker charts to show who had partnered with whom, and new partners were chosen randomly, using lolly-sticks (those again!) to ensure a range of peer-work experience.

OK, some teachers had to employ special stick-picking techniques again, this time because certain pairings might very well have sent them over the edge – if you know what I mean.

Quick Question: Do your pupils have the opportunity to work with a wide range of partners?

Before the new pairing, children were encouraged to evaluate their current talk partner or buddy in terms of support, help and peer-buddy skills. Having growth mindset established meant that our children were able to listen and take on board their peers' comments, and the evaluations enhanced their understanding of themselves as reciprocal learners. All of this had set us in good stead for one of the integral aspects of our Fast Feedback approach: the cooperative review. This technique has children critiquing one another's writing according to the toolkit. There are guidelines for this, which you can read about by skipping straight to Chapter 6, but again I must stress that laying the foundations and developing the right learning culture will increase the chances of it being done successfully and having a positive impact.

Ownership of learning

Although the idea of Fast Feedback started with the need to reduce teacher workload – and it most certainly does – for teachers to give up written marking, I'm sure you agree, children must be in the right place. They need to be more independent and more self-regulatory. They need to feel responsible for their learning journey in partnership with the teacher. Children need to 'own' their learning.

Imagine children who know how to learn: who manage distractions, who are resourceful, who can work with others or alone, who ask good questions, who notice things and learn from others, who can see links and understand their own learning. Why then shouldn't those children be able to assess and mark their own work? Or evaluate a partner's work? Surely it would be a travesty for all that knowledge of learning to go to waste by making a teacher spend hours and hours putting pen marks all over children's books. We thought so! We weren't totally crazy, so we decided to do a trial 'no marking' (of maths and English) before making it whole-school policy. Before you are treated to how that went, here's a quick reminder of some of the key points we've covered in this chapter:

Chapter Summary

- If children already have a voice in their learning, moving towards self-marking will be smoother.
- If children practise the skills of learning and know themselves as learners, they will become more self-regulatory.
- Policies are more likely to be followed if you ensure that all staff (including new staff) understand the pedagogy behind them.
- Too many new initiatives close together will increase workload and are less likely to succeed.
- Developing good peer/partner work can promote metacognition.

5 Trial and tribulation
Developing the approach to Fast Feedback

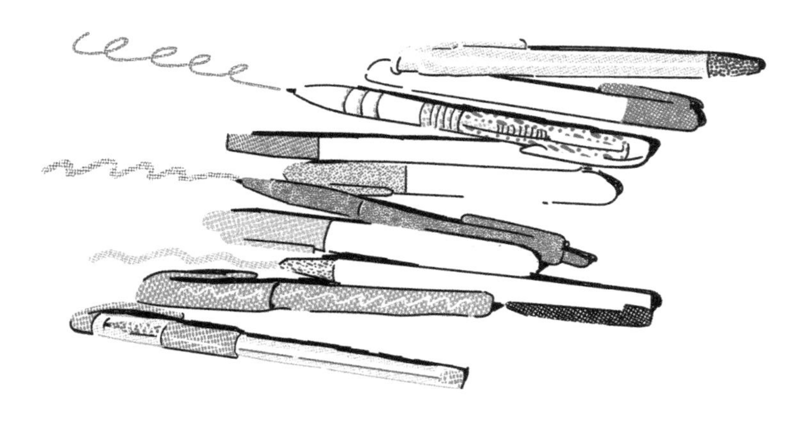

Once upon a green pen

Many, many years ago, the buzz around schools was how wrong it seemed to cover a child's hard work with red pen. 'Red is harsh' and 'red is such an angry colour'. We were 'burying' their work with corrections and comments, which (it was said) could destroy their self-concept. And what was the answer? To change the colour of the pen! Some schools changed to blue; many went for green.

Let us take a moment to consider what the real issue was. Personally, I believe we were devaluing any learning that had taken place by putting our own stamp on it, by turning it into someone else's work – the teacher's maybe? All the corrections to spellings and punctuation and all the suggestions for better vocabulary made it far more about the teacher than the child.

If you are a leader you will be used to 'book scrutinies'. I've done hundreds of them over the years. What is it that you see in those books? Curriculum content and coverage is definitely something to be looking for, but far too often my team and I would see, first and foremost, the teacher's handwriting. If it wasn't neat enough – a good model – we weren't happy. Then we might read the teacher's comment and be impressed with how in-depth it was, how much it picked up on the positives and highlighted areas to develop. If it didn't, we were not happy. Then the follow-up tasks: did they match the target or missing toolkit item? If not, you guessed it – we were not happy (in fact, I'd almost have a hissy-fit if the date was missing). What was happening here? We were judging the children's learning (the quality of the teaching) on a teacher's ability to write the correct things in a book (neatly). We needed to be able to see progress from one piece of writing to the next, but how on earth could we see that progress if it had been buried by teacher text?

Fast Feedback allows you to see progress. It allows teachers and leaders to see the children's work, their corrections, their reflections on themselves as learners, and the learning that happens during a pupil–teacher conference.

Quick Question: What do leaders 'see' during a book scrutiny at your school?

The truth about marking

Book-looks can be time-consuming and draining for leaders. But being a teacher during a book scrutiny is really tough. Again, honesty is my policy and I'm going to admit to something now from the safety of retirement. Back when I was a class teacher, total panic would set in when word got round that A was on her way to collect some books for a random scrutiny. You see sometimes, *because of workload*, the marking wasn't always up to date. Teachers – you get that, I'm sure. Leaders – you may have forgotten how hard it was (I certainly did as a leader). So, with the impending doom of A appearing at the door, I'd grab my trusty green pen and fill in any gaps as quickly as I could. Shameful, I know. And what could I scribble in such a short time that would be guaranteed to get me out of a potential pickle?

The letters VF.

VF is marking shorthand for 'verbal feedback', which was allowed back then. Not always, mind – only on occasion. However, it was seen as an acceptable way of correcting misconceptions and steering learning in the right direction.

I'm going to repeat that:

> *Verbal feedback was seen as an acceptable way of correcting misconceptions and steering learning in the right direction.*

Hey, it's just taken close to a decade for everyone to fully appreciate this. Please don't bin the book in disgust at my admission. Firstly, verbal feedback would have happened, so it wasn't entirely dishonest. Secondly, there are more juicy confessions on the way.

When I was a Year 1 class teacher, one whole day of my weekend was set aside for planning, resourcing and marking, as was almost every weekday evening. I'd spend hours writing comments, corrections and follow-up tasks in my very best 'infant' handwriting in the hope that the children could read them. A lot of the time they couldn't. Even the higher achievers might want something explained and I'd end up with a class full of waving 'read it to me' arms. I was forced to take action.

I developed two strategies to try to minimise this madness. One was to send off those children who *could* make sense of what I'd written to start on their follow-up task. Then I'd keep the rest on the carpet whilst I quickly read my comments and next steps to a group – sending them off a bunch at a time. There was no ownership, and it was a complete waste of valuable learning time.

The second strategy I employed was very brave for the time. This was before growth mindset and learning to learn and way before the idea of no marking. This was when teachers were expected to focus on one group at a time: 'The Focus Group'. So, five groups in a class (always aptly named but that's another book), one group a day, the whole class in a week. How neat. Set the others off on learning (hah!) and you sit with your focus group and do some intense teaching. No flitting or helicoptering – that was very naughty. But there was still the problem of the marking. What *I* would do was set my focus group off on their task, then I'd scoot around the class, explaining here, correcting there and clarifying everywhere. The whole time I was terrified that a senior leader would walk in and catch me – God forbid – teaching.

To salvage just a little bit of a life beyond school, I got even more cunning. After whispering advice, exploring and rectifying misconceptions, and pointing out corrections to be made, I would (shame upon shame) quickly write what I'd just said in their books. I was marking books during the lesson! There I said it – I suspect that some of you did this too and might still be doing it if you're a 'marking' school. It wasn't the type of marking during the lesson that even I would frown upon – you know, the teacher puts on a video and sits at the back marking books (and yes, I've witnessed that level of desperation). No, what was happening here was pupil–teacher conferencing. This was 'live marking', which is how some people describe a form of Fast Feedback; but it was very much against the rules back then.

I'm not the only one to have flouted the rules and I must thank people for their honesty during research interviews. At the beginning of the 'Big Marking' nonsense, when teachers were expected to do all that highlighting, one rebelled. Natalie, our brilliant Reading Recovery teacher at the time, took a Year 5 group for English once a week:

> *I refused to do the Big Marking highlighting. I remember thinking, 'Why am I spending all my time doing this? The children should do it so that they can see what they've achieved!'* (Natalie)

Rules and policies are usually made with the best of intentions. However, we know that sometimes they become counterproductive. We wanted our exciting new initiative to work for teachers and children, so for our summer 2016 trial of 'no marking' (we'll discuss the name later), the rule book was practically thrown out.

The trial

Although there were no rules as such for the trial of no marking (except, of course, 'don't mark the books'!), there were three simple non-negotiables:

1. You must look at the books.
2. You must provide verbal feedback.
3. You must allow children time to self-assess and reflect.

The two teachers chosen for the trial were excellent teacher-leaders – one Year 2 and one Year 4. Let's consider the non-negotiables we gave them, starting with 'you must look at the books'. I've come to realise over time that some people falsely imagine that not marking means not looking at the children's work.

Quick Tip: Be prepared to deal with the misconception that not marking means not looking at the children's work – you'll be surprised how common it is amongst parents, governors and other stakeholders.

However, for the two teachers doing our trial (indeed any teacher), looking at the books is a no-brainer. Why wouldn't they? Why wouldn't they want to see how the children had got on with a task or lesson they'd planned and delivered?

The next, 'giving verbal feedback', shouldn't really have caused too much of a problem for them either. They were both outstanding AFL practitioners and were incredibly thorough when giving feedback – marking like there was no tomorrow. Not a book was missed. Not a comment was left out. Every word written was specific to the individual child. The feedback was brilliant, but I have to stress that it was 'written'. The non-negotiable of 'verbal' feedback was tricky for them, as the very act of cutting out the writing caused some anxiety. Gemma was one of those teachers:

> *We were both quite heavy markers at the time and took a lot of pride in our books. I remember I was anxious about it initially – the change in what I was used to but also the idea of books looking 'unmarked'.* (Gemma)

I'll admit that we had a strong feeling that those two teachers would find it hard not to write in books. Did we choose the heaviest markers for this trial on purpose? Yes, we did.

The difficulty with letting go of marking is not unique to Lavender's trial. Recently I was talking with a group of teachers who were trialling the introduction of minimal marking for their school. Although they were coping quite well with going cold turkey, and were keen for it to become policy, they were adamant that 'so-and-so' would never go for it: she'd never be able to get off the pen. It is a big change to put down the marking pen. Even though marking can mean hours and hours of time away from your family and your life outside work, it is embedded in the culture of being a teacher. Teachers mark work, and to stop marking almost feels like removing part of your remit as a teacher – taking away your professionalism.

Quick Tip: If teachers are struggling to let go of the pen, remind them that the profession is about enabling pupils to make progress. Teaching is not about writing in books.

I've seen teaching described, in a dictionary, as an 'interactive process to help someone to learn'. How interactive is it to give children heaps of green comments a whole day, or even longer, after they made their efforts? How meaningful is it to the children? How efficient is it in terms of teacher time? Why do we do it? My thoughts earlier about written marking becoming more about how leaders judge a teacher's worth was confirmed for me recently by Nicola:

> *During the trial, one of my worries was, 'what evidence will I have to show that I've looked at the children's books?'* (Nicola)

The evidence is in the children's progress – simple. Even just a trial of 'no marking' then was a cause for anxiety, but we were lucky to have a blessing from on high. A few months before our trial, in March 2016, the advice from the Independent Teacher Workload Review Group (2016) was:

> *...if your current approach is unmanageable or disproportionate, stop it and adopt an approach that considers exactly what the marking needs to achieve for pupils...* (Independent Teacher Workload Review Group, 2016, p. 10)

When children can't read, or properly understand, the written comments, and the teacher has to spend time explaining the misconceptions and next steps anyway, then time is being poorly managed. Why not just talk to them? When trolleys and cases full of books are being wheeled home every evening, or the school is kept open late for Big Marking, then marking workload is disproportionate: disproportionate to the time spent on actual teaching and to the time spent having a life.

The quotation above advises adopting an approach that is right for what schools want pupils to achieve. We wanted them to make progress, not just in conceptual understanding, knowledge and subject skills, but to make progress as effective learners. We had a vision of children taking the tools of learning with them into secondary school and onwards. We wanted children who knew themselves as learners, confident learners, for life. Ah... dreamy maybe, but why shouldn't they be?

Quick Question: Does your school's approach to marking support what you want for your children?

The final non-negotiable, 'you must allow children time to self-assess and reflect', also caused some worry. Lavender pupils were used to self-assessment and, with the second wave of learning to learn, were beginning to be more reflective about their learning. However, this wasn't as embedded as it might have been. There was a genuine worry that young children might not be able to evaluate and reflect upon their own work and learning in any meaningful way; we'll look at how to address this a little further on.

How to support children in writing honest, useful reflections was just one of the points explored, along with many others, at regular meetings between Lavender staff. Our partner school, Brimsdown, was carrying out its own trial of 'no marking' at the same time, so we also had mutual feedback sessions with them. Quite a few of the concerns, questions and decisions raised at both schools were similar, but that didn't mean the outcomes were exactly the same. In Chapter 7 you'll see how schools have reduced or eliminated marking in slightly different ways, but there are two key consistencies: firstly, development of the right learning culture, and secondly, a trial period before rolling it out across the school and other subjects. Carefully choosing teachers, year groups and subjects for a trial, holding regular feedback and discussion meetings with teachers, leaders and support staff, and even getting the voice of the children about the approach will help to ensure buy-in and success with Fast Feedback. That's not to guarantee instant success. There will undoubtedly be wrinkles along the way (we certainly had to iron out a few, as you will see) but you will put yourselves on a better road to reduced workload and lifelong learners.

Creating guidelines

The wrinkles raised during our trial period were many, but as Gemma so beautifully put it during our analysis of that half-term, 'Well, with every trial comes tribulation.'

All right, the problems, concerns and questions raised didn't cause intense heartache, but they may have increased staff anxiety when going 'whole school' if we hadn't looked for answers during the trial. One of the early concerns was whether there should be consistency around a number of points: a prescriptive policy. Should every class do it in exactly the same way? The teachers only had those three non-negotiables, remember, so were free to try whatever methods they wanted to give feedback to their children and record the outcomes. Having a Key Stage 1 and a Key Stage 2 class in the trial meant there would end up being slight differences in approach anyway and we knew that the age and needs of the children would determine some of the methods used in the scheme.

We found ourselves laying down some rules after the trial, but (remembering all the problems that our previous expectations documents caused) we created the Fast Feedback expectations as a 'guide'. We had a consistent message of 'what to do' but not 'how to do it'. (Except, and I'm sorry about this, which colour pen to use for different bits.) We felt that, sometimes, clearly defined guidelines and trust in teachers might be the better way. You can see the complete document in Chapter 6, Figure 6.1.

Autonomy and monitoring

Earlier, I discussed the link between marking and teacher monitoring, and would like to remind you of Nicola's concerns about evidence. She was worried that not marking children's books would mean there would be no evidence that she was looking at their work. As a teacher, I worked hard to give my classes the best possible education and have always seen teaching as a labour of love. The small minority aside, I believe that teachers go into the profession for the right reasons: they genuinely want to help children. Sadly, these professionals can end up feeling that they're not trusted to do their job because they are watched, monitored, scrutinised and directed to distraction (later on, I share how we have tried to address this by introducing Fast Feedback for teachers). Leaders can feel the same way (I hear the resounding 'yes' from you, I do) but although schools must, without doubt, be held accountable, that shouldn't mean that teacher autonomy has to be stripped away. When you strip away any autonomy, I think you strip away some of the joy of teaching.

One of the questions around autonomy and monitoring raised during the trial was whether there should be a certain style and amount of record-keeping and whether leadership should see it. We already had an online assessment tracker at the time, which, along with unadulterated children's books, should have shown us all we needed to see in terms of children's progress. The format and content of teacher notes, we decided, should be up to them.

Quick Tip: To avoid stripping away autonomy, allow teachers to choose how they record their discussions with children.

Both Gemma and Nicola, it turned out, kept copious notes during the trial. Notes so extensive that the workload pretty much matched that of marking the books! This eased off as they got used to not marking and they both developed their own workable systems. When we became a no-marking school, other teachers also felt the need to make copious notes, but soon developed easier ways of record keeping. Such systems included gap-analysis tick sheets (using printouts from the assessment tracker) and class lists with learning outcome headings and space next to each name for quick notes. In Figure 5.1 you can see an example of one teacher's notes made after conferencing children for maths.

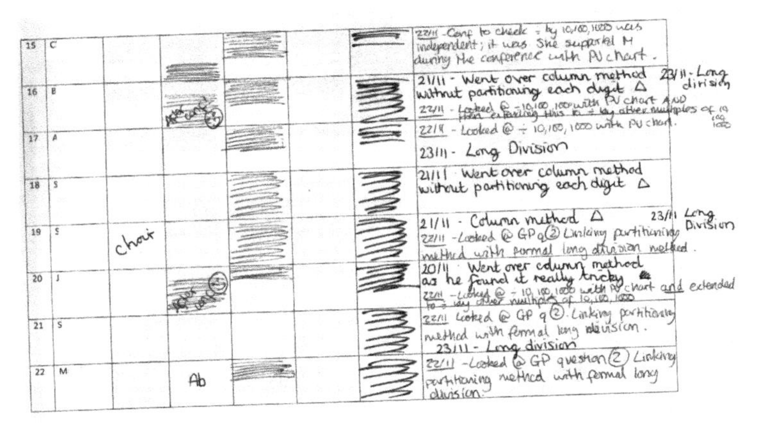

Figure 5.1 *A teacher's notes on the learning and needs of the class may contain scribbles, emoticons and highlights. The format should be what works for each individual teacher.*

You can see a further example of teacher notes in Chapter 7. Approaches were, and still are, different. The important point here is that of ownership.

Another point that came up during the trial was whether there was a need to produce a written plan for the verbal feedback conference. Again, we felt that this would just create more work for our teachers, so decided it should be optional. A conference is good, interactive feedback. If, after looking at a child's work, you see that they need to use commas correctly, then discuss with them where commas should go and why. That doesn't need to be in a written plan. However, it is appreciated that, just as 'how we learn' can differ between individuals, so too can how we approach our teaching. Some might prefer to write things down first, especially at the beginning, to help organise their thoughts and to ensure that the feedback they need to give is focused and effective. But expecting a written plan for every conference (of which there will be many) will add to workload. Marking books might then start to look like a better option – a familiar one!

Quick Tip: To avoid increasing workload, writing conference plans should be optional.

Reward and motivation

We were asking teachers to stop the familiar. To stop doing something that was embedded in the view of themselves as educators. Teachers are used to being judged on their marking, on their planning and on their delivery. We were taking away judgement of their marking and perhaps, then, an opportunity for validation. I guess we all need to know that we're on the right track and, to varying degrees, need proof that we're doing a good job. For teachers, there are plenty of other ways – including the most important: children's progress. Children too were used to seeing those comments in the books, validating their efforts. They were also used to seeing pretty stickers and smiley faces. To sticker or not to sticker became a key topic of discussion during the trial. One of the arguments was that if teachers were no longer writing in books, to then add a smiley face or 'well done' sticker (without the context of feedback) would make this (token) marking even more meaningless to the children and wouldn't necessarily increase motivation. You can explore more on the theory behind these ideas in this chapter's fact file on reward and motivation.

FACT FILE: REWARD AND MOTIVATION

What

A reward is something given to someone to recognise their effort or achievement. Motivation refers to a person's willingness to engage or persist in a task or their reasons for behaving in a particular way. As most reward systems aim to motivate people, there is a significant relationship between the two.

Why are reward and motivation important to Fast Feedback?

Integral to our approach is the development of children as lifelong learners. Stickers or empty praise might motivate in the short term but (alongside excellent planning and feedback) encouraging children to evaluate and recognise their own efforts and achievements can increase intrinsic motivation and help lead to lifelong learners.

Key people

Edward Deci

Edward Deci is known in psychology for his theories on intrinsic and extrinsic motivation. He is co-founder, with Richard Ryan, of self-determination theory, a contemporary motivational theory.

Key messages

Rewards

There are two types of reward often used within schools to recognise achievement or reinforce behaviour:

Intrinsic reward

- An intangible award of recognition or sense of achievement that comes from within a person (internal).
- Includes genuine contentment with completing a task.
- Pupils do something because they enjoy it or find it interesting.
- Can be linked to self-determination theory: people are motivated to grow and change when their needs for competence, connection and autonomy are fulfilled (Ryan and Deci, 2000).

Extrinsic reward

- A tangible and visible reward physically given to an individual for achieving something (external).
- Includes stickers, certificates and even praise.
- Pupils do something because they seek the reward.
- Can be linked to operant learning theory: rewards (as positive reinforcement) lead to repetition of desired behaviour (Skinner, 1938; 1953).

Intrinsic vs extrinsic motivation

- According to Daniel Pink (2018), human beings are deeply motivated by autonomy, collaboration with like-minded colleagues and work that matters to them.
- Reward-focused incentive systems intend to motivate or reinforce student learning; however, though widely used, their effectiveness has been questioned.

Deci, Koestner and Ryan (2001)

- Deci, Koestner and Ryan conducted a meta-analysis on the effects of feedback on motivation and found a negative correlation between extrinsic rewards and task performance.
- They concluded that tangible or extrinsic rewards can have a 'substantial undermining effect' on a student's motivation to learn and their interest, persistence and autonomy (Deci et al., 2001, p. 1).
- In his earlier work, Deci also found that when the anticipated reward goes away, we perform the rewarded behaviour even less than before. Working for a reward could actually overwrite any original motivation and reduce how much you do it (Lepper et al., 1973).

Motivation is also a key factor of Claxton's Learning Power approach (see Chapter 4) and children's interest in 'learning to learn'.

Claxton

- Advocates that children need to be intrinsically motivated to be effective at metacognition and reflecting.

- Those that are extrinsically motivated are 'interested only in getting marks, grades and praise' and gain little satisfaction from having mastered something tricky or produced something they are proud of (Claxton, 2018, p. 4).

Deci's findings are also concurrent with research conducted by Hattie and Timperley (2007) and their 'model of feedback to enhance learning' (see Chapter 6).

Hattie and Timperley

- Found that feedback linked to praise, extrinsic rewards and punishment is least effective for enhancing achievement; rewards should not be thought of as feedback at all.
- In their 'model of feedback to enhance learning', feedback given at the 'self' level, involving personal evaluations about the learner, is rarely effective.
- Praise for task performance is also ineffective as there is little learning-related information provided (Hattie and Timperley, 2007).

Can praise and rewards be of value?

Some research would suggest that extrinsic rewards can be effective when used in specific ways.

- According to Willingham (2007), rewards can work if they are enticing (high value) and given immediately (to minimise the time between effort and gain).
- Tangible rewards could also help with concrete learning goals such as learning multiplication tables. However, in

accordance with Deci, rewarded behaviour tends to stop when the rewards stop (Willingham, 2007).

- Others have suggested that verbal praise can increase intrinsic motivation, and whilst tangible rewards given to individuals simply for doing a task can have a negative effect, overall, reward does not decrease intrinsic motivation (Cameron and Pierce, 1994).

Putting it into practice

For leaders

- Provide training for all staff so that they understand the theory behind using reward for motivation and encourage teachers to share tips for motivating their pupils.
- Ensure the school policy on reward is clear and linked to research, and that it provides consistency for children and staff to avoid confusion.
- Use whole-school reward systems, such as marbles in the jar or house points, for a specific purpose and ensure it is of value to the children.
- Consult trained colleagues on the use of reward systems and what is valuable for individuals, the class and whole school, but also ensure staff have autonomy to decide what works for them and their children.

For teachers

- Talk with your class about their learning and encourage them to make connections about the decisions they make now and their long-term goals.

- Provide feedback on pupils' understanding and how they learn best, but encourage pupils to do most of the talking.
- Ensure praise is specific and focuses on the process rather than the outcome or the pupils themselves.
- Encourage pupils to persevere with a task to see what happens; make it part of the classroom culture to enjoy and be interested in the outcome.
- Provide children with meaningful work and projects that aim to spark intrinsic motivation; the more they enjoy a task, the more motivated they will be.
- Use extrinsic rewards sparingly for specific goals, not as feedback, and ensure they are immediate and of value to the children.

Key quote

'Kids are capable of intrinsic motivation... So why do we distract the children in our care with sticker charts, time-outs, and treasure box troves that have no clear connection to learning?' (Minkel, 2015)

Further reading

- Minkel, J. (2015), Distracted by rewards: moving beyond carrots and sticks, Education Week, www.edweek.org/teaching-learning/opinion-distracted-by-rewards-moving-beyond-carrots-and-sticks/2015/03

  (An interesting article written by an elementary school teacher about moving beyond extrinsic motivation)
- Pink, D. H. (2018), *Drive: The Surprising Truth About What Motivates Us*. Edinburgh: Cannongate.

  (For insight into how to motivate ourselves and direct our own lives)

- Smith, J. (2017), *The Lazy Teacher's Handbook*. Carmarthen: Crown House Publishing.
  (Includes ideas on phrases to use to improve motivation)

We eventually agreed that we wouldn't put stickers in books, but that teachers could sticker as part of the reward system already in place in their class. Most classes were adorned with fancy charts, or even rockets to the Moon, to show children how great they were. We also had gem jars across the school, which, when full, earned the class a treat. Add to that the values certificate assemblies and the house points system and it's safe to say that, despite what research might say, there was extrinsic reward aplenty!

Good-quality verbal feedback given during teaching and conferences should be enough and would be far more meaningful than a sticker. However, some children's need for written praise for their hard work or success hit home a few weeks after we introduced Fast Feedback across the school. I'd sent out a questionnaire to find out what the children thought about teachers not marking their books anymore and one of the headings asked what they didn't think was so good about it. An honest response from a Year 6 child can be seen in Figure 5.2.

It has taken time to develop the Fast Feedback culture at Lavender. We introduced a huge shift in practice that would benefit the teachers, in terms of workload, and the children, in terms of learning. Some aspects of our learning culture were already securely in place, whereas others needed work: children needed to understand that a real smiling face with a worthwhile comment was better for learning than a drawn or sticky one.

Quick Tip: Have meta-learning discussions with your children around the difference between good feedback and a sticker/ well done comment. Get them to consider how each might affect their learning and progress.

What I don't think is so good

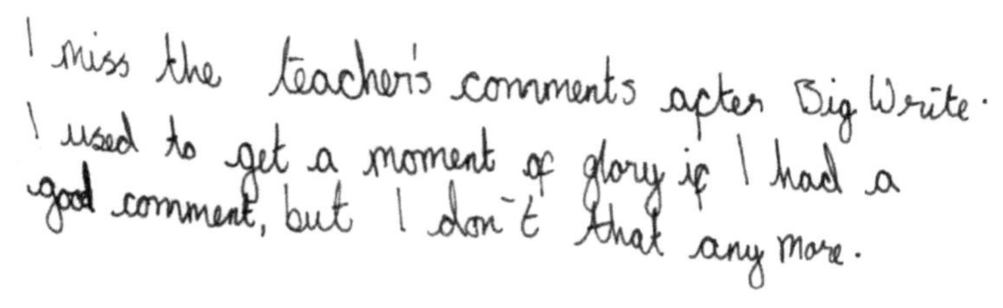

Figure 5.2 *Don't underestimate a child's need for praise and glory. This Year 6 child gives his honest opinion on Fast Feedback.*

Encouraging reflection

The sticking of other things into books also became a regular discussion point. As mentioned earlier, there was worry that some children might not be able to reflect on, or evaluate, their work in any meaningful way. Children doing their own toolkit ticking and maths marking is enlightening for teachers, without a doubt. But the reflections on themselves as learners, how they approached a task, how easy or hard they found it, and what they feel they need to do next are gold dust.

However, 'I enjoyed it' and 'I worked hard' were not really what we were hoping for. OK, so very young children do say things like this to begin with, but it truly wasn't that bad – I'm being over-dramatic. Still, we did need to encourage good reflections and Gemma and Nicola came up with some ways to do this. Amongst the ideas were speech or thought bubbles, or frames, in which children could write what they had learned and their thoughts about what they needed to do next. It is incredible how much time we spent trying to decide whether to have fluffy thought bubble clouds or speech bubble shapes and the whole thing became a bit of a red herring. Regardless of which was the best, we were at a point where the trial teachers were spending a ridiculous amount of time cutting out bits of paper and sticking them into books. Dragging ourselves back to the fact that the trial existed because of teacher workload, we all agreed that the solution needed to be easy. Enter the reflection prompt mat.

Quick Tip: Sentence starters on the whiteboard or 'mats' on the table with questions and prompts are a simple way to support children in writing reflections on their work and learning.

The mats saved the day. After self-marking, our children now choose a prompt or two and reflect on their learning. Simple. This not only keeps workload down, but also ensures 'in-depth' reflective comments from our children.

Sentence starter and question mats for various subjects are readily available online. They include useful prompts such as:

What I need more help with is…

A strategy that helped me was…

One thing I need to remember from today's lesson is…

Next time, I will make sure…

What helped me when something got tricky was…

I would now like to learn more about…

An example of a science prompt mat, developed by Gemma during the trial, can be seen in Figure 5.3.

Conferencing

The trial also raised the question of whether teachers should pre-plan which children to conference each day, or whether it should be more spontaneous. The overwhelming opinion at our meeting was that conferencing should depend on need. If, when looking at the books, a teacher identifies that a child has not 'got' something, then clearly that child needs a conference during the next session. There were concerns raised that conferencing might end up being all about the

Figure 5.3 *Sentence starter mats can be subject-based, as is this science one, or can contain more general prompts on learning – a simple resource that helps children to reflect.*

lower-achieving children. However, with cognitive load theory in mind (check this out online if you haven't previously had a chance), along with properly differentiated planning and clear, concise teaching, all children should be challenged at the right pitch for them. Therefore, conferences would be for everyone: for catch up or consolidation.

When we disseminated the scheme across the school, several teachers struggled with finding the time to conference every child, especially during practical lessons such as science. We'd initially asked for a set number of conferences per unit or session, but we needed to adapt this, especially for foundation subjects. For those, and for science, we decided that each child needed at least one conference per 'topic' or 'unit'. Other schools have different expectations, but the key message is that conferencing has to be manageable, and it has to make a difference. One of the biggest challenges you may encounter as a leader or teacher in a no-marking school is how to ensure all the children are being conferenced, or are given feedback, as and when they need it.

Lavender teachers and leaders found various ways around this challenge. These included fitting in conferences during assembly times (you will have your views on this), as 'early work' (we had 'soft-start' at Lavender, where children could come into school up to 15 minutes before official start time) or during other lessons where there was classroom support. There were, however, two key strategies that were essential to making Fast Feedback conferences work. The first one might seem obvious, but at the time of rolling out no marking across Lavender, we found that we had to confirm with staff that it was OK to do this. It is simply to hold 'group conferences'. Often, a number of children might need the same lesson, be it the reteaching or embedding of a previously taught concept or a 'greater depth' lesson to challenge and move on the learning. This group could be a pair, trio or more. It is essentially the same as the old 'guided group lesson' or like the 'group conference mark' mentioned in Chapter 1, but now far more fluid and flexible. When teachers look through the books, they can make piles of similar need, gather those children into a group and teach them. This is active, responsive teaching.

Quick Tip: Work as a school team to find and agree ways that ensure all children are being conferenced as needed, without affecting their education in other areas.

The next way around the challenge was for us, as leaders, to clarify what we meant by a conference. Two weeks into being a no-marking school, we held a staff meeting and added this to our expectations document (there were cool pictures too):

Conference definition (Dictionary)
A formal meeting in which many people gather in order to talk about ideas or problems related to a particular topic (such as medicine or business), usually for several days.
Conference definition (Lavender)
A more formal meeting (than helicoptering) when two or more people gather in order to talk about ideas or problems related to a particular topic (such as learning), usually for several minutes.

Helicoptering *is giving instant feedback, keeping them on track, making them think. Though sometimes mid-flight you spend a little longer with a child and they say some deep stuff about their learning!!! Let them follow it up with* **a sticker** *if you need it captured or you need them to consolidate what they just said.*

Doing our job properly and letting teachers know that helicoptering could be accepted as a 'mini conference' was ground-breaking. Not only was 'flitting' allowed, but it was expected! I love to be honest, for your benefit: if we'd thought to do this earlier, we'd have avoided a lot of anxiety for our teachers.

Hmm, I hear you saying, with suspicion, 'What's this sticker thing? I thought they were a no-go!' Don't worry, our Fast Feedback stickers were not for reward; they were there to support the children's learning. During the trial, we'd all realised that teachers couldn't possibly remember the ad hoc, unplanned conferences and the teaching points that came from them, let alone *which* children had had a conference. We also knew that the children needed a way to embed and remember those teaching points. We came up with two stickers:

I spoke with my teacher and...
I spoke with my friend and...

They went into the book after a conference or peer review, the child completed the sentence and voila! Two examples, one from a maths book and the other from an English book, can be seen in Figures 5.4 and 5.5.

Spelling errors

You'll notice that the child writing in the English book in Figure 5.5 has self-corrected 'discussed' and has a delightful way of spelling 'hyphens'. You may be wondering at this point how teachers will

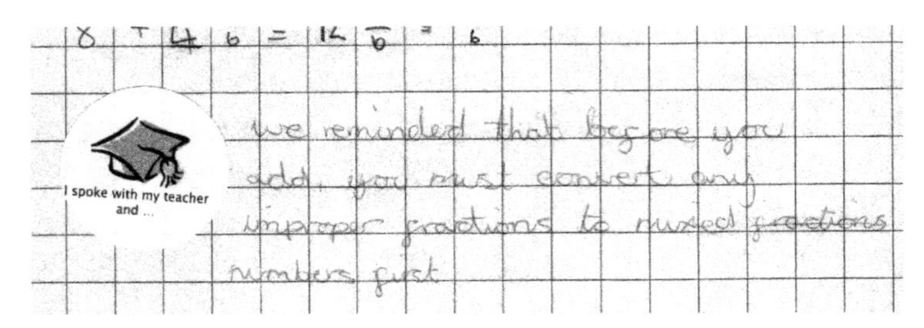

Figure 5.4 *A quick conference and reminder, followed by the sticker comment, will have helped to consolidate learning for this child.*

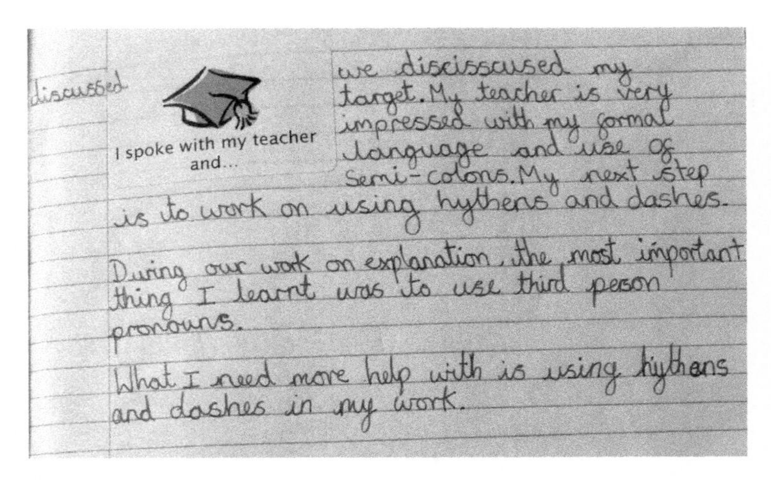

Figure 5.5 *Through conferencing, this child has developed a keen awareness of their own strengths and learning needs.*

highlight spelling errors if they can't write in the books (this is a common question asked of us about Fast Feedback). In the old days, when a child's work was covered with teacher pen, the spellings were often corrected, along with the punctuation. In the (very) old days, the child might see those corrections, maybe say 'oh' and probably move on. We'd developed spelling journals some years before Fast Feedback, with the idea that teachers and children choose some of the spelling errors to put in the journal to practise. But time to do this in the lesson wasn't always available. With Fast Feedback, the humble 'sticky note' made its debut.

As teachers look through the books, they pick out key spellings, pop them on individual sticky notes and place them in the books. The children then transfer the sticky note to their spelling journals and use all the fabulous strategies known (taught) to them to learn to spell that word.

Quick Tip: If you want to challenge children further, give them a sticky note with a number (keep it reasonable), which is the number of key spelling errors within the piece that they need to find, check and correct themselves (using a dictionary).

The trial findings

This chapter set out to be about the trial we carried out before telling everyone to stop marking, but in fact many of the strategies mentioned, such as the spelling sticky notes, were implemented during the early stages of the roll-out. I guess it has all been a trial that has needed tweaks and changes to make it work for our school. Hopefully, some of the solutions we found will help you to avoid the same mistakes, as will the many problems we had to solve during the whole-school launch (which you're about to find out about). Nevertheless, at the end of the 'official' trial, we did feel we'd identified the best way forward. So again, for your benefit, a quick recap on the findings and messages highlighted in this chapter:

Chapter Summary

- Unadulterated children's books give a better picture of their progress than those covered in teacher pen.
- Being tied to set groups on set days can mean missed teaching opportunities.
- Letting go of written marking, for some teachers, will feel like a threat to their professionalism.
- Some elements of Fast Feedback will need to be optional.
- Reliance on extrinsic reward could hold a child back from developing as a truly effective learner.
- Children will need help and support to write worthwhile reflections on their learning.
- Conferencing can take different forms and can happen at different times.

6 Rolling it out *Fast Feedback across the school and community*

The excitement of the new

The last trial meeting was long. We went round and round in circles trying to make final decisions about whether to use stickers or stamps, bubbles or forms and, yes you guessed it… what colour pen the children should use. At the time, the children were writing in blue (if they'd earned a 'pen licence', that is; otherwise it was pencil), the teachers were marking in green and the children were doing response tasks in purple. As you can imagine, it was all very vibrant. During the trial, Gemma and Nicola had decided to let the children do their own marking and reflections in purple. Should it be purple then? It was late in the summer term, it was hot, and we were all getting tired when Matthew had an idea. 'I think they should correct their work and write their reflections in green – the colour that the teacher uses. The teacher can then ceremoniously hand over the pen to the child.' Comments of approval and endorsement flew around the room and boy we were smug (again).

Our smugness was short lived (keep reading – major quick tip coming up in this chapter!).

We were so excited about the new term. This was it; the whole school was going to stop writing on children's work. We had our non-negotiables (don't write in books, look at books, give time for reflections, carry out regular conferences, set targets with children) and our first ever Fast Feedback expectations document, see Figure 6.1.

Teachers would now be facilitators of learning. They would give feedback to children at the right time, in context, and it would be meaningful. There would be no more nonsense of children not understanding what the teacher has written. There would be no more slavishly filling children's books with words.

Ofsted

Naturally, we were also a little anxious about the whole school moving to Fast Feedback. Ofsted was still just around the corner (they'd been around the corner since 2012, remember) yet we'd told our teachers to eliminate writing in children's books. However, if we were taken to task about this, we had a comeback at the ready. The March 2016 workload document, referred to earlier, also included this little gem:

> *Ofsted does not expect to see any specific frequency, type or volume of marking and feedback; these are for the school to decide through its assessment policy. Marking and feedback should be consistent with that policy…* (Independent Teacher Workload Review Group, 2016, p. 9)

Let's just distill this, the way we did back then: as long as our policy says 'no marking', they can't tell us off for not marking. Without doubt,

HOW WE DO FAST FEEDBACK at LAVENDER

Fast Feedback works because we have a culture of Growth Mindset and Learning to Learn
These expectations must be read alongside our Teaching and Learning Policy

1. All work is acknowledged through conferencing/discussion/immediate feedback
   - Conferences are planned into each unit. They can be held as individual subject conferences or combined
   - Maths and English in-depth conferences are held for each child at least once every 2 weeks in classes of 30, once a week in smaller classes
   - Science conferences should happen at least once every unit and more often if the unit is longer than 4 weeks
   - Foundation subject in-depth conferences held for each child a minimum of once per unit of work
   - On the spot feedback happens as much as possible!
   - High expectations of presentation are paramount and presentation must be referred to regularly
2. The teacher/cover teacher keeps a record of which children have had conferences to ensure every child has the minimum required
3. Teachers (including supply and cover support staff) keep a note of the key feedback points given to support planning and assessment
4. Books and pieces of work are checked every day to inform planning for the next lesson
5. Cover staff make notes and sort books for the teacher, to inform planning and assessment
6. Target Tracker is used regularly to highlight statements and for gap-analysis planning
7. Planning allows time for children to draft and craft their work and to carry out follow-up tasks
8. Self/peer reflection time is built into all lessons to enable children to consider what they have learnt, how they might improve and what their next steps might be. This might be at any appropriate point in the lesson and can occur more than once in a lesson as mini plenaries - there is no expectation of an old-style 3-part lesson!
9. LOs are explained to children at the beginning of each unit of work to give the big picture and to frame the lesson success criteria and relevant targets
10. Success criteria forms the basis for effective feedback and children are encouraged to create the success criteria with teacher support, as appropriate
11. There is always a toolkit/steps to success/clear success criteria for the child, peer and teacher to refer to
12. Work (including follow-up work) is done with either pencil (for maths in particular) or blue pen
13. Feedback is specific and about improvements that can be made – not just what's wrong or right
14. Targets are reviewed regularly (during each adult/pupil conference)
15. New targets are set through discussion and the child is encouraged to become increasingly independent at considering own learning needs and next steps
16. Children reflect on adult/peer/own feedback then consider their targets and follow up tasks, with support where appropriate (younger children might be given a choice of pre-set follow up tasks to choose from)
17. Self-reflections are written on thought bubbles (younger children) or straight into books (older children)
18. Self-reflection mats are often used to provide response stems
19. Digging deeper comments are written straight into books in green pen
20. Teacher conference reflections are written on sheets (younger children) or straight into books (older children)
21. Marking stations are set up, in maths lessons, for children to check their own work (these may be on tables)
22. Children mark and reflect on their work with a green pen either with peer/adult support or by themselves
23. Homework does not need written feedback as it involves learning spellings, number bonds and tables, etc. It also involves visits and activities which the children can speak about (see homework expectations)

2016

Figure 6.1 *Our first ever Fast Feedback expectations document will have undergone a few tweaks over the years to make it work better for us.*

the quality of the feedback given is key to learning and progress, and we'll be looking at that shortly, but the threat of an Ofsted visit shouldn't be a reason to not stop marking. Nevertheless, it has been one of the major concerns raised by school leaders during our Fast Feedback professional conferences.

Worry not, for the quote about Ofsted from the Independent Teacher Workload Review Group report (2016) has been put to the test. Brimsdown Primary School, who trialled no marking at the same time as us, were actually 'Ofsteded' during the trial! (I'm sure 'Ofsteded' will make it into a dictionary soon.) Here is what was said:

> *Leaders have not been afraid to adopt innovative approaches to increasing pupils' rates of progress. For example, teachers make effective use of pupil conferences; they meet individually with pupils to ensure that teachers have a clear picture of what pupils understand, and that pupils are clear about what they need to learn next...* (Ofsted, 2016)

Both Lavender Primary School and Brimsdown Primary School have had successful Section 8 inspections since embedding Fast Feedback, so please don't let concerns about Ofsted put you off creating a great learning culture and reducing teacher workload.

Data

We didn't just have Brimsdown's Ofsted during the trial to give us the confidence to 'go with it' the following September. We also had data (see Figure 6.2).

SUBJECT	TRIAL GROUP	CONTROL GROUP
Reading	4.6	3.19
Writing	10.95	-1.6
Maths	4.2	3
Combined	9.35	2.7

Figure 6.2 *Although this was a short-term study, the trial data was encouraging. To stop writing in children's books appeared to be having a positive impact on outcomes!*

Figure 6.2 shows increases in the percentage of children reaching age-related expectations (ARE) during that half term. For each year group the percentages were higher in the classes taking part in the trial compared to those classes that were not taking part in the trial. Obviously, it was a short-term study and the numbers were small, but the data was encouraging. (If you're wondering why the impact was so much greater in writing, some believe it to be because 'maths ownership' was already more embedded at that time.) Indeed, more recent data from Ivy Learning Trust shows improved outcomes for schools that are using the Fast Feedback approach.

Children respond to the trial

The data was important, without doubt, but the children's responses to the trial sealed the deal for us. One of my favourite parts of the morning when delivering a professional conference to schools on Fast Feedback is showing the video of Paige from Year 4, sharing her opinion of 'no marking'. The sincerity of her little speech is both convincing and delightful. If you've time, pop over to the Ivy Learning Trust website (ivylearningtrust.org) and see the video for yourself. Otherwise, here is a transcript (please imagine sincere gestures, such as hands on heart, and facial expressions):

> *The no-marking policy is good because we get to reflect on all our work and if we've made a couple of mistakes here and there like, umm, don't put a comma in or don't use a capital letter, we can use our purple pens, which I really like, to correct it and that's quite good, especially in drafts. And the other thing I like about it is we get to have, like, our own books. It just feels like they're 'us'! And, umm, say I had a drawing pad with my name on it, yeah? I feel like that's mine to use freely as I want. That's how I think all of us feel with our books.*

Paige's words highlight a couple of things. Firstly, how important it is to let children draft and change their work. How often are you able to write a perfect version of something the first time? We need to cross out, change and add to our words, or rub out lines and shading and develop our art. It also highlights how Fast Feedback was a final step in children's 'ownership' of learning. They'd always had their own books, but now they truly belonged to *them*, not to the teacher.

Quick Question: Do children at your school feel that they 'own' their books?

The Year 2 video interviews also confirmed that we were about to do a good thing. We received the following feedback on English:

> *When my teacher was marking in my book, I found it difficult to read and understand what to do. Now, as my teacher is speaking to me more, I find it easier… what to do and understanding.* (Year 2 child, with English as an additional language)

And on maths:

> *Before, the teachers marked it and we had to wait a day to see if it's correct. But now we just correct it with our purple pens and move on to do a harder challenge if we got it right.* (Year 2 child)

Taking stock

It was evident from their feedback that the pen colour was important to the children. As mentioned, we'd decided to go with green for the children. It was very symbolic. The teacher relinquishing the pen. The child taking up the pen.

It was the third day of the autumn term; two days of INSET had ensured that our teachers were ready to 'not mark'. Gemma and Nicola had done fabulous presentations, the non-negotiables had been presented and Jodie had done some creative training on effective feedback. Teachers were ready. The children were back.

As headteacher by then, I was in my office doing some of that stuff that headteachers do (you know, trying to turn the budget black, making an action plan for those people who were 'just around the corner', and so on) when one of the office team told me we had a problem.

'No one ordered any green pens.'

That's why the smugness mentioned earlier was short-lived and here's the major tip I promised: know someone with an Amazon Prime account. (We did and the face of leadership was saved.)

Effective feedback

It was a new dawn, a new term and children had their marking pens. The teachers did Fast Feedback, and the feedback was effective because of Jodie's INSET. You can read the theory around effective feedback in this chapter's fact file.

FACT FILE: EFFECTIVE FEEDBACK

What

Feedback is information provided by an agent regarding aspects of a learner's performance or understanding; it aims to bridge the gap between what is understood and what is aimed to be understood (Hattie and Timperley, 2007).

Why effective feedback is important to Fast Feedback

Our approach will reduce teacher workload and improve children's outcomes. We know that much written feedback can be ineffective and take up hours of a teacher's life. Verbal feedback can be immediate and done within the school day, but it can also be ineffective if not done properly. There is much research about what good feedback should look like and, in order for Fast Feedback to work, it is essential that teaching staff and leadership have this training and understanding.

Key people

John Hattie

Professor John Hattie is a researcher in education and proponent of evidence-based teaching. He is well known for his books on Visible Learning (Hattie, 2009; 2012) and research into effective feedback.

Key messages

Hattie's Visible Learning study

- Hattie conducted extensive meta-analytic work of research relating to teaching and learning.
- To find out what works best in education, he ranked various influences according to their effect on achievement measures, from very positive effects to very negative.
- Feedback was found to have a very positive effect, demonstrating significant impact beyond developmental effects and typical teacher effects.
- He concluded that feedback has a critical influence on student learning and later referred to it as the most powerful educational tool available for improving student performance (Hattie, 2009).
- However, the study also showed variability, with some types of feedback having more effect than others.

Feedback about a task and how to do it more effectively has the highest impact (Hattie and Timperley, 2007).

What is effective feedback?

- Providing and receiving feedback requires skill from both students and teachers.
- For the greatest impact, it needs to be combined with effective teaching and learning strategies (Hattie and Clarke, 2019).
- Feedback must be clear, purposeful and meaningful and compatible with pupils' prior knowledge, to support them to make logical connections between ideas; timing, resources and the classroom climate must also be considered (Hattie and Timperley, 2007).
- Hattie and Timperley's model of Feedback to Enhance Learning (Hattie and Timperley, 2007) can be used to support teachers and pupils to give effective feedback.

Purpose

'To reduce discrepancies between current understandings or performance and a desired goal.' (Hattie and Timperley, 2007, p. 87)

Discrepancy can be reduced by

Students:
- Increased effort, motivation and employment of more effective strategies that lead to understanding.
- Abandoning, blurring or lowering the goals (less productive).

Teachers:
- Providing appropriate, challenging and specific goals.
- Assisting students through effective learning strategies and feedback.

Effective feedback answers three questions

1. Where am I going? (What are the goals?): Feed up
2. How am I going? (What progress is being made towards the goal?): Feed back
3. Where to next? (What activities need to be undertaken to make better progress?): Feed forward

Each feedback question works at four levels

Task level
How well has the task been understood/performed: correct or incorrect?
- Best when it results from faulty interpretations, not lack of understanding.
- New material/surface knowledge.
- Can involve less cognitive effort.
- For example: Does the answer meet the success criteria? What did you do well? Where did you go wrong?

Process level
What strategies are needed to understand and perform the tasks: are there alternatives?
- Best when it provides direction and strategies for error detection and forming relationships between ideas.
- Some degree of proficiency needed.
- For example: What strategies did you use? Why is the answer correct/incorrect? What could you do differently?

Self-regulation level
Self-monitoring and regulating of actions to achieve a goal. Internal feedback, self-assess and less reliant on peer or teacher feedback:
- Willingness and confidence to invest effort leads to further engagement, ability to evaluate; know when to seek and respond to feedback.
- High degree of proficiency needed.
- For example: How could you monitor/check your own work? What could you now teach to someone else?

Self level
Personal evaluations (usually positive praise) about the learner:
- Often used but rarely effective.
- Students may minimise effort and avoid risks if feedback is negative.
- For example: Good boy, well done.

Task, process and self-regulation levels are all interrelated: the aim is for children to question and reflect on what they understand and seek feedback that allows for the best opportunities for learning (Hattie and Timperley, 2007).

Brook's eight steps towards feedback for learning (Hattie and Clarke, 2019, p. 6)

Brook further summarises effective feedback in eight steps:

1. 'Sparks learning'.
2. 'Flourishes in the right environment'.
3. 'Clarifies for students where they are going'.
4. 'Informs students how they are going'.
5. 'Highlights the next steps for improvement'.
6. 'Matches the needs of the learner'.
7. 'Promotes students' self-regulation'.
8. 'Flows bi-directionally between learners and teachers'.

Criticisms of Hattie's Visible Learning meta-study

It is worth mentioning that Hattie's Visible Learning research is not without criticism. Critics have argued that (summarised from Killian, 2015):

- There is too much focus on pupils' academic results.
- Effect size is not a valid measure to use.
- It relies heavily on meta-analyses and the findings are overly simplistic.
- Low-quality studies were included in the research.
- Findings should not be seen as a checklist for improving schools.

However, Visible Learning is still widely acknowledged as one of the most significant summaries of educational research ever conducted.

Other findings

The EEF's Teaching and Learning Toolkit (EEF, 2018), based on a summary of international evidence on teaching five-to-16-year-olds, also supports the importance of effective feedback on outcomes:

- Feedback was rated high impact for very low cost, based on moderate evidence.
- Educational studies identify positive benefits where it is effective but it should:
  - Be specific, accurate and clear.
  - Compare what a learner can do now with what they have done before.
  - Encourage and support effort.
  - Be given sparingly but meaningfully.
  - Provide specific guidance on how to improve.
  - Be supported by professional development for teachers.

When feedback isn't effective

- Though delayed feedback can work for more complex processing, the more immediate the feedback the better (Kulik and Kulik, 1988).
- Sometimes reteaching or other strategies are needed, not just feedback alone.
- The level of difficulty is optimal: the learner needs background knowledge and skills to respond to feedback successfully (Bjork and Bjork, 2020).

- It is not just about 'giving' feedback – feedback about what they know and understand is most powerful from student to teacher (Hattie, 2012).
- Assessments and tests provide minimal feedback – teachers must devise activities and questions that provide feedback about the effectiveness of their teaching to know what to do next (Hattie and Timperley, 2007).
- It is important to get feedback right: when it works, the sender achieves the desired changes and the recipient can adapt and learn; when it doesn't, it can be counterproductive, cause withdrawal and defensiveness and damage relationships (Sutton et al., 2012).

Putting it into practice

For leaders

- Provide training for all staff on giving effective feedback and encourage teachers to share experiences and tips.
- Encourage teachers to learn from each other through peer-to-peer observations.
- Ensure children are explicitly taught how to give and receive feedback and that this is regularly recapped.
- Share strategies for giving effective feedback with parents and caregivers: feedback happens at home too!

For teachers

- Coach pupils to receive and act upon feedback by teaching explicitly and modelling regularly.
- Focus on quality – how much is understood and taken on board – rather than quantity – how much and how often feedback is provided.

- Use tools and templates to promote effective peer feedback, such as the 'cooperative review', and ensure this is a collaborative process (rather than just swapping books).
- Following a conference, ensure children can reflect on the feedback given: can they understand and apply it within their work? If not, is further explanation required?
- Allow for individual differences between pupils: some may need more motivation and support to respond to feedback and criticism.
- Ensure that any praise given is specific, timely and related to the learning rather than to the pupils themselves.
- Encourage pupils to do most of the talking and give feedback on their understanding and how they learn best.

Key quote

'That students are taught to receive, interpret and use the feedback provided is probably much more important than focusing on how much feedback is provided by the teacher, as feedback given but not heard is of little use.' (Hattie and Clarke, 2019, p. 5)

Further reading

- Education Endowment Foundation (EEF) (2018), Teaching and Learning Toolkit, https://educationendowmentfoundation.org.uk/evidence-summaries/teaching-learning-toolkit/feedback *(For the full evidence-based summary and ideas for giving feedback)*
- Hattie, J. and Clarke, S. (2019), *Visible Learning: Feedback.* Oxon: Routledge.

(For recent research and expertise into the practicalities of feedback, including variability of feedback, peer-to-peer feedback and creating the right culture)

- Hattie, J. (2021), Visible learning: What works best for learning, https://visible-learning.org

  (For articles, videos and further information about visible learning and effective feedback)

Jodie's presentation of the theory around effective feedback was both innovative and delicious. We were treated to YouTube clips of Paul Hollywood giving *Bake Off* contestants their dreaded feedback and we explored what impact it might have on the learning of the bakers. We considered the importance of specific feedback whilst describing mirror glazes, and we pondered process feedback whilst eating cake. If you'd like to eat cake at your effective feedback training, I believe Jodie is available.

What is key here is that conferencing with children as an element of Fast Feedback isn't just about pointing out the missing commas. As highlighted previously, following secure AFL-based planning, it should then be a conversation around where punctuation belongs and why. It is also a conversation about children's understanding of punctuation and how they can be helped, and help themselves, to use it correctly and for effect.

Quick Tip: Pupil conferencing will work best when lesson planning is done within a culture of formative assessment, and when there is a good understanding of what effective feedback looks like.

The Education Endowment Foundation's (2021) third recommendation for good feedback is 'plan for how pupils will receive and use feedback'. Don't worry. This principle doesn't conflict with the idea of helicoptering if the teacher is trained to understand what good feedback looks (indeed sounds) like. However, if the quick, unplanned conferences become just about what is wrong or missing from a child's work, that is simply not good or effective.

The Teacher Workload Review (2016) document asks for marking to be meaningful and motivating. Process-level feedback can motivate children, enhance deeper learning and lead to self-regulation, yet trying to have a meaningful discussion on how the success criteria has been met or exploring a child's strategies and encouraging children to seek feedback can be very difficult to do at home with a pen. Fast Feedback's immediacy can increase children's confidence to seek feedback, which is something wonderful to witness – although it can be scary too.

What's in a name?

We were two weeks into the autumn term and a teacher in Year 5 needed an impromptu meeting with a parent. As a headteacher, you don't get to do much cover (all headteachers of small schools now protesting loudly), so I felt a little apprehensive.

'Of course, what are they doing?' I'd asked, worried that I'd have to introduce a concept that I hadn't brushed up on. It was maths. They'd had their input and they were working on their independent tasks. The answers were on the tables. What could go wrong?

I was in the classroom for five minutes when 'S', a high achiever, called me over. 'Ms Hill, I'm not sure about this. Could you give me a quick conference please?'

First thought was, 'Wow!' Then, 'Oh ****, I've never actually done a conference myself', and suddenly it was a little scary. But it was fine. I gave feedback and I did some one-to-one teaching. Why was I scared? Because even though I'd championed the approach, I'd not done it myself. Or rather, at that moment, I thought I hadn't. But I'd given one-to-one feedback for years. I'd taught for years. I'd eaten cake and done the effective feedback training. The irrational anxiety came from the fear of something new.

The 'conference' label was new. The name 'Fast Feedback' was also new. We understood that calling the initiative 'No Marking' might cause problems; specifically, parents assuming that teachers were binning their responsibilities. So, Matthew asked staff to come up with ideas for a name and Stuart, a Year 3 teacher at the time, gave us Fast Feedback. Although the Fast Feedback approach is really about good, effective teaching, the introduction of a new 'named' initiative can be scary.

I spoke with one of the teachers who found the introduction of Fast Feedback daunting to begin with. Although she hated marking, and Thursday nights were 'hell', she admitted that completing the marking of all those books gave her satisfaction – a sense of achievement – like she'd done her job properly (this reinforces the idea discussed earlier, that there is an unwritten rule that to be a teacher, a real teacher, you must mark books). When the leadership team at Lavender announced that teachers wouldn't be marking books anymore, Katie was horrified and admitted that she'd almost had a mini breakdown:

> *I'd been marking for almost 18 years. I felt that it would take away everything I knew about teaching and assessment, and I kept asking myself, 'How will I know the children?' I also felt out of my depth as the less experienced teachers seemed to take to it so easily. It was threatening to me as a professional, I suppose.* (Katie)

This worry about making it work wasn't unique to Katie. Although we'd provided expectations, we'd been adamant that we wouldn't impose strict rules about how those expectations were to be met. We were so keen to trust teachers that we'd not considered how leaving them to find effective systems and routines that they liked caused them workload!

Dealing with roll-out issues

No marking was meant to reduce workload and we were confident, following Gemma and Nicola's positive feedback from the trial, that it would. Once they'd got used to keeping briefer notes, they found that the time saved on marking was huge and their personal lives were hours in credit. However, the roll-out, as mentioned earlier, ended up being a trial too, which impacted on some teachers' confidence and workload. There were, in fact, all sorts of issues and questions that popped up over the first month of whole-school Fast Feedback, which caused many a wrinkled brow. We knew we had to do something.

As you know, we weren't a leadership team to offer a detailed, prescriptive list of dos and don'ts and, as we'd not done a longer, wider trial, we didn't know the best dos and don'ts anyway! Also, some of us hadn't been 'on the shop floor' living the new strategy, so why would *we* have the answers? The answers had to come from teachers who had already discovered ways to smooth out wrinkles, so I devised a game to play during a staff meeting. The teachers sat in groups, and each was given a sheet of paper with two columns, one headed 'my problem/worry/concern is' and the other headed 'you could try this/I did this'.

This is how it works: each person writes a problem or concern and passes the sheet to their left. Each person writes a possible solution to the problem they've just been passed, folds over the paper, and then adds another wrinkle of their own. Keep writing, folding and passing to the left, going round the group a couple of times if necessary. A bit like the consequences game.

The sheets were gathered and the collated results shared with all staff. Actions were taken and everything became more manageable. The teachers had the experience and the knowledge – they just needed a forum to share. Table 6.1 shows a slimmed-down version of the collated findings, which may be of help when introducing Fast Feedback.

Table 6.1 Fast Feedback – peer support, 31 October 2016

My problem/worry/concern is...	You could try this/I did this...
Managing the behaviour of the rest of the class whilst doing conferences with children.	Make sure planning is tight and children have prepared tasks – DD/NRICH extensions. If I finish...
Helping LA children whilst sat with a group.	Give appropriate task and resources for LA so they can manage independently.
Resources issues slow us down.	Order more pens by letting Sue B know.
Peer-assessment stickers time-consuming to hand out to whole class.	Keep stickers on the table.
Children not being able to write in each other's books.	Verbal? Stamper to say verbal feedback? Sticky notes?
Peer/self-reflection still not great.	It will come with practice. Have 'stems' available and 'think aloud' replies to help them.
Not always able to discuss targets for target sheet.	How does your work today link to your target? Conference stems.
How to conference with a group of children who will not talk about their learning.	Scaffold conversations using open/closed questions, visuals, thumbs up, traffic light to start conversation.
Lessons not suiting conferencing (worksheets, drama, adult-led).	Worksheets with tick boxes for children to self-assess against (always a toolkit).
Linking all feedback to targets.	I don't think all conferencing can be – perhaps focus when possible or do a guided group if moved on.
I forget to write up notes and now the time has passed, arghh!	Have a tick list! Y6 have monitors in groups to take notes for you.

How to do detailed conferencing in English when there are so many misconceptions.	Make a list of children with greatest need and try to group them. Then note smaller issues on sticky notes for children to try and address.
Unsure whether children grasp the concept of reflection in Reception.	If you start early they will adapt.
Still writing 'she told me'. Mixed ability pair reflections not as effective as independent.	Use possible sentence starters (perhaps on display in the classroom).
Children completing good work and not having a 'good' comment.	Give a verbal 'good' comment.
If you're off sick, pulled for cover, person covering not who was expected and notes not completed or conferences carried out.	SLT to remind cover staff of expectation.
Ensuring off-track children are supported (daily).	Provide strategies/visuals for the children. Have the 'opportunity' to pre-teach the children to ensure they are engaged during the lesson.
Conferencing the same children over and over because they need extra support – so not getting round everyone.	Get children to support each other. Strategically pair them – train children. Look at level of challenge for these children – maybe work too hard?
Not having enough time in lessons to do everything.	Do reflections and I spoke with the teacher all at the end.
Not enough time to conference in French with only 30 minutes a week and mostly practical whole-class activities.	Children to complete self-assessments and address children with any worries/concerns.
When you go in as cover it's difficult to get FF fitted in beyond reflection.	Spend last 15 minutes doing a whole-class conference/review of their learning.

Conferencing in subjects other than maths and English once per topic/term.	Take a week and do all conferencing aimed at that subject.
Knowing when it is a guided group or a conference, and whether reflection could be done in both?	I would not worry too much about this. If a child/group of children have had additional support/teaching based on AFL, put a conference sticker in and get the child to reflect.

As I was cutting and pasting the comments in Table 6.1 from the original document, it struck me again how valuable this exercise was. Because the answers came from class-based colleagues, and were based on experience, they had far more validity than leader directives.

Quick Question: Do staff in your school have a regular forum to share practical ideas around teaching and learning?

You'll find more answers to your worries about potential problems in the coming pages and knowing some solutions will certainly save you some work. However, there is no guarantee that you won't encounter your own unique obstacles when implementing Fast Feedback in your setting. I give the same advice as I gave about Ofsted: please don't let wrinkles put you off creating a great learning culture and reducing teacher workload.

Parents and carers

For Lavender, it wasn't just class teachers and support staff who had Fast Feedback wrinkles. The leadership team also had to smooth a few. We'd anticipated parental concern following the news that teachers weren't marking anymore, so we took pre-emptive action by sending out a letter at the end of the summer term. Here it is:

Dear Families,

Following the successful trial of our no-marking initiative last year, which showed children making outstanding progress, we would like to share with you our plans for feedback from September.

A change in practice means that teachers will no longer write in children's books and a more effective style of 'Fast Feedback' will be happening across the school.

Children will be given the opportunity, at the end of each lesson, to review their work, correct any mistakes and consider what they have achieved or what they need to work on. We will also encourage children to write self-evaluation reviews at the end of lessons, to give teachers insight into the child's own understanding of their learning.

Whilst it means that teachers will not be writing in children's books, they will, of course, be monitoring the children's work and books continually throughout lessons and will be giving effective oral feedback and guidance, through 1:1 and group conferencing.

This change in practice will promote self-regulation, independence and lifelong learning. It also, of course, supports the Lavender learning culture of Growth Mindset and Learning to Learn.

Should you have any questions, please do not hesitate to speak to your class teacher or any member of the leadership team.

It worked. There were no phone calls of horror to answer; everyone seemed fine with it. The letter was undoubtedly a good move, but I don't believe it was that on its own that got families on board. I'm going back to ethos now. From my very first day at Lavender nearly 20 years ago, I could see that family involvement was an embedded and valued part of the culture. This never wavered and, during the years running up to the introduction of Fast Feedback, we'd held countless events for parents, carers and families, such as drop-in days, science fairs, reading mornings, curriculum evenings and training sessions (including growth mindset!). Parents were on board because they felt informed and included. I believe that this helps to promote trust.

Quick Question: How might parents and carers at your school feel about teachers not writing in books? What would you need to do to get them on board?

None of us are so arrogant that we believe school is the only educator. We know the importance of parental involvement and the impact on learning, especially when carers can't support their children's education. We must believe that we, as individuals, can make a difference but shouldn't underestimate the importance of involving families.

With all this in mind and being honest (again), there was something missing from the letter that might affect parents and carers. A wrinkle (or three) that we'd not thought through properly. We'd directed teachers to stop writing in children's books and they came to us, rightly so, with three key questions.

Handwriting

The first question teachers asked was,'Can we still model handwriting in their books?'

We remembered Paige's comments about her books so agreed that modelling should be done on paper, or on a whiteboard, for children to copy. Confession here: this question set us on a path of realisation that handwriting lessons weren't happening as regularly as they might have been and handwriting at Lavender wasn't great (actually, it was rather atrocious, and we'd been trying to sort it out for years). Once, before I knew any better and in desperation, I taught a handwriting style in a staff meeting and then insisted that all marking was done in that style! (This is my opportunity to say sorry. I was a class teacher too at the time and *so* regretted that directive.) Eventually, we found an online scheme that was not only incredibly easy to use (and cheap) but it transformed handwriting across the school, almost instantly. I kid you not; my jaw was permanently on the floor as child after child was sent to my office with their writing books. I wouldn't name the scheme here, and I'd imagine there are others that are just as good, but one of the attractions was that families could download it at home – for free. This helped to both give ownership to the children and include parents and carers in their learning.

Quick Tip: If you need a new handwriting scheme, find one with an online version that families can access too – for free.

Reading records

Another question that linked to parents and carers was: 'What about writing in home reading records?'

I don't know about you, but I've seen home reading records or journals used as communication vehicles for things that have absolutely *nothing* to do with reading. This is especially true in the Early Years, where comments such as 'Can you make sure he eats his lunch' and 'Sorry about the odd socks' are as common as 'She loved this book'. We knew that ownership of learning was as important in reading as in any other subject, so it was an easy decision.

Unless children were unable to copy a book title and author name themselves, teachers and support staff would stop writing in reading records. We expected children to write reflections on what they'd read: how much they enjoyed it, what page they were up to, how difficult or easy it was. Parents could transcribe for those who weren't able to do this, or the child could use an emoticon to express their thoughts. Staff were always available at the end of the day for conversations with families, and morning messages (about socks and lunch) were welcomed in the office. Again, this doesn't mean that teachers stopped looking at the reading records. Children's thoughts and comments provide insight for the teacher, and they work as a discussion starter during group or one-to-one reading sessions. We even introduced a sentence starter rubber stamp for reading records, similar to the stickers for writing books, saying, 'I read with my teacher and…' to elicit responses, such as 'I used my inference skills to understand the children's actions'. (Some no-marking schools *do* still write in home reading records, and we explore this more in Chapter 7.)

By the way, I must admit that some children clearly weren't reading at home, so the naughty extrinsic reward popped up to 'sticker' the sweatshirts of every child who commented in their reading journals. It worked short term and gave us space to identify what else we needed to do to encourage home reading.

Homework

The third question teachers needed an answer to was: 'Do we mark homework?'

Hmm, this was a meaty one which led to very long discussions and a whole new policy. We'd talked (staff *and* parents) for what felt like years about the rights and wrongs of no homework or too much homework. The old 'it will prepare them for secondary school' had reared its head regularly, and 'they're at school all day and need time to be children' was there too, along with all the valid points about children's mental health and wellbeing. If we continued with the homework route, it had to follow our policy on no marking. What did we expect children to do outside school? One of the homework elements that we retained was the practising of key skills. Children are expected to learn maths facts, such as bonds, tables, fraction–percentage equivalents, and so on. They also continue using their journals to embed spellings and spelling patterns, and they 'read'. None of this needs marking. All of it is valuable learning.

We could have continued to dish out task and activity sheets as well but let's be honest: do we ever really know how much help a child has had? When marking those sheets, we couldn't truly rely on the data and use it as part of our assessment for learning approach.

Quick Question: If you send home problem/question sheets, how much of what is marked feeds into children's assessments and planning for next steps?

If the sheets were just for children to use as practice, and the data wasn't reliable anyway, why were we marking them? To validate this type of homework, we could have asked for more conferencing and discussions about the help needed and so on, but we decided against it. Year 6 teachers were a wee bit anxious about this, so maths practice questions went home regularly, but were marked as a class the next morning. That aside, we cancelled 'homework sheets' and saved the planet (and our budget) from hundreds and hundreds of pointless photocopies and our teachers (and indeed support staff) from hours of meaningless ticking.

So, apart from the things mentioned above, what does our policy ask for? It's simple. It asks children to research an upcoming topic or theme and to bring their findings into school. Because the titles are so open, such as 'Enfield Town', children can access them and deepen their learning according to their own starting points. On Home Learning Day (when parents are invited in and classes visit one another) you might see children carefully manoeuvring a model volcano, clutching a home-made booklet about local history or using a USB stick to present a slideshow on chocolate. They might just have a crumpled sheet of notes that have been prepared for a 'lecture'. The name-change to home learning meant that families felt encouraged to work and learn alongside their children. Yes, some children will need support from adults in our homework club and yes, some volcanoes are obviously created by parents, but that's OK. Children still go on to share their project findings with others and the day gives teachers valuable information about children's presentation skills (not always easy to assess). Children are also encouraged to self-evaluate their presentations and learning, as well as to peer-assess their classmates. The homework has true meaning.

Quick Tip: 'Home learning' days promote parental involvement, give meaning to homework and offer a vehicle for developing and assessing children's speaking, listening and presentation skills.

Peer reviews and feedback

Peer reviews and feedback are important aspects of our no-marking strategy and are used across the curriculum. But it's not just about hearing what a friend says is right or wrong and following their advice. As a no-marking school, we ask children to look at one another's work against a set of criteria, and to discuss with their partner *how* those criteria have or haven't been met. The pair will then consider possible improvements, different approaches and next steps. It is not about just saying whether the outcome is correct or incorrect.

I opened a child's sketch book soon after we'd introduced Fast Feedback and read, 'I spoke with my partner, and we thought that I should put more shading and detail on the petals.' A couple of thoughts popped into my mind. The first was sheer delight that the peer feedback was happening in art too, as it should. The second delight was seeing the word 'we'. It was clear that a discussion had taken place and that they had agreed on positive steps forward to improve the work. Peer 'feedback' is not simply assessment; it is a two-way conversation. You may now be asking, 'But what if that conversation had resulted in "I spoke with my partner and we thought that my drawing was great", but it wasn't?'

A common concern raised at our professional conferences is how 'correct' self and peer reviews are. If one child's advice to another is wrong, then there are steps to take. The child giving the wrong advice needs a conference to address misconceptions. The child receiving the wrong advice needs a conference to clarify their understanding and to address any misinformation. Wow! This sounds like a lot of extra work, doesn't it? After all, you could just spend a few hours marking all the books correctly yourself. But which is the most productive use of effort? Peer reviews are teaching opportunities. They provide a forum for training in dialogic talk and in giving and receiving effective feedback. They help to develop analytical and evaluative skills in *both* partners. When the peer conversation ends with, 'I hear what you're saying but I think it works better if I leave it as it is because…' (as the child refers to the toolkit), then you'll truly see its worth.

Quick Question: Are children in your school taught how to review one another's work?

Cooperative review

One of our most effective Fast Feedback strands is the 'cooperative review'. This idea was brought to Lavender by Natalie, after she'd attended a Pie Corbett and Shirley Clarke course back in 2014. As part of her literacy INSET on the benefits of in-lesson quality feedback (yes, *in-lesson feedback, two years before Fast Feedback!)*, Natalie promoted strategies such as reading work aloud to develop a 'sense of audience' and the use of visualiser stops. During a visualiser stop, a child's work is shared on screen to invite class feedback and to highlight good examples, which will move learning on *whilst* it is happening (obviously, growth mindset helps here). She also advocated partner feedback, or the cooperative review.

Lavender's cooperative reviews happen after Big Writing. Partners work on one book at a time with the author, or partner, reading the work aloud. They discuss one another's work and decide whether the toolkit items have been met, ticking against the success criteria. The partners discuss good things in the writing, and they consider next steps. An absolute *must* is that the author holds the pen and writes the outcome of the peer reflection. The ownership is still with the author, and it is the author who decides what to write in their own book after this (or any other) discussion. An example can be seen in Figure 6.3.

Group work and reflections

Whether spot on or 'not really getting it' (and we'll look more at that in a bit), children's reflections add immeasurable depth to a teacher's understanding of where pupils are in their learning. One area that truly showed the value of reflections was that of practical group work. Excellent, well-planned group activity lessons were widely used across the curriculum at Lavender, yet how could teachers really know how much learning went on during them? A popular technique across the school was, and still is, to stick photographs in the children's books of them 'doing' the activity. There would be a title, a date and a learning outcome. Such pictures can help to prompt the teacher's memory when carrying out assessments and they provide useful evidence that a learning activity has taken place. However, a picture of a group activity stuck into a book, *followed by a child's reflection on the learning that has taken place* gives the image true worth (see Figure 6.4 for an example).

So, that well-known phrase 'a picture is worth a thousand words' is not always true! A reflection, however, *is*. Not only is a reflection a wonderful insight into children's understanding, but those people around the corner like it too:

> *Teachers encourage pupils to reflect on their learning and become independent thinkers.* (Lavender Ofsted report, 2020)

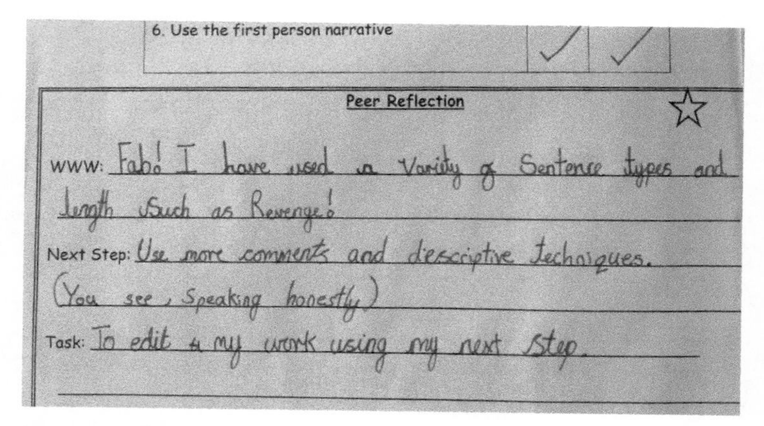

6. Use the first person narrative	✓	✓

Peer Reflection ☆

WWW: Fab! I have used a Variety of Sentence types and length Such as Revenge!

Next Step: Use more comments and descriptive techniques. (You see, Speaking honestly)

Task: To edit my work using my next step.

Figure 6.3 *This cooperative review (or peer reflection) uses a 'what went well' (WWW) prompt to encourage recognition of learning achievements, as well as next steps.*

The true value of a reflection

Let them reflect. Children know how they found the work; they know how much of a challenge it was – whether too easy, too hard, or just right.

If they know, give them the time to express it. As with all self-assessment, in any curriculum area, there must be clear learning outcomes and success criteria, as highlighted in our cake-eating feedback discussion earlier. But, if a child achieves the learning outcomes and the analysis becomes all about 'I got it right, it was easy', clearly more challenge is needed, along with some support in writing reflections. If it was 'just right', consider other prompts to further develop reflection skills, such as: 'Which strategies did you use to get to that answer?' or 'Which learning skills did you draw upon to complete this activity?' Move on the metacognition so that the reflection is about the learning, not about the activity.

Like peer reviews, you may be worried that some self-reviews might be wrong. Let's clear this up. If you have a culture where children are honest about their learning, if they understand that reflection is a good thing and have been trained to be (constructively) critical of themselves and others, then the reflections and self-marking that you see will be an invitation into children's heads. If a self-assessment is wrong, then the child either doesn't have the right mindset and can't be honest about their own learning (in which case that needs work) or the child hasn't grasped the concept/learning outcome (so that needs work). In a nutshell, the child needs a conference. A wrong self-reflection can be as valuable as a right one.

Well, I'm sure you are champing at the bit to encourage children to reflect on their learning (if they're not already). However, a little word of caution. Remember the children's questionnaire we sent out a few weeks into Fast Feedback? Remember the honesty of one child who was missing the 'moment of glory'? Well, another child wrote this:

What I don't think is so good:

'I don't like it because it is so much work and I can't take it anymore.'

We got carried away. I admit it. In fact, even though the children were overwhelmingly positive about Fast Feedback, many thought that there were just too many reflections. Lavender was proud of its work around children's mental health and wellbeing, so we knew that we had to find a better balance. You can have too much of a good thing.

Quick Tip: Be mindful of not overwhelming children with too many extra tasks when introducing a new initiative.

The other thing you may be keen to do is to reduce your teachers' workload. Of course you are, or you wouldn't be reading this book! So does it actually work? After Brimsdown School's trial, they were able to produce a brilliant set of data that showed an actual reduction in the hours spent by teachers writing in books. At Lavender, we hadn't done such a study, but I think the quotes below from some of our teachers help to confirm the benefits of banning marking:

Figure 6.4 *This child's reflection on a group activity provides valuable insight into how they have approached and understood the learning task.*

I'd like to experience another school in the future, but it would have to be a no-marking school. (Molly, teacher at Lavender since qualifying)

The amount of time saved allows me to be more creative with planning and resources. (Teacher who wanted to use her creativity)

I can't bear the marking. I never appreciated how much time it takes. I don't have a life at the moment. (Teacher who had only known Fast Feedback and then moved to a marking school)

This [no marking] is one of the reasons I described my starting at Lavender as 'finding the oasis in teaching'. (Charlotte, who came from a marking school)

And my favourite:

I can't commit to co-writing the book until the summer holiday. (Gemma, trail-blazer and co-author of this book, who moved out of the area and now works in a marking school)

Reduced teacher workload and better learners. What more can you ask for? OK, you're probably asking for more, like, 'How will Fast Feedback work in my school?' or 'I want answers to specific questions'. Keep reading for those answers – after this chapter summary:

Chapter Summary

- Ofsted is fine with Fast Feedback (in fact they liked it).
- Fast Feedback led to better outcomes.
- Children's views on a new, or existing, approach can be gold dust.
- Feedback must be 'effective' – training is key.
- Roll-out can be daunting. There will be teething problems and staff should work together to find the solutions.
- Inform parents before roll-out and involve them whenever you can.
- There is no need to write on *any* children's work.
- Reflections – as an individual, as a peer and after group work – are all incredibly valuable.

7 What about us?
Making Fast Feedback work in different ways

Fast Feedback – a summary

In this chapter, I'll answer some of the queries raised at our professional conferences and also let you know how some schools have adapted elements of Fast Feedback to suit their settings. Before that, I think it will be useful to do a quick recap.

- Our 'no-marking' approach depends on the learning culture that we have embedded: the values, behaviours and skills that support the right mindset and ownership of learning.

- Assessment for learning and clearly defined success criteria allow children to mark and evaluate work alone, with an adult, with a peer or with the class.
- Children are taught to reflect on the work, commenting on their understanding, successes and difficulties, and are challenged to consider their approach to the learning.
- Reflections are a window to children's understanding, not just of concepts, but of themselves as learners. They provide teachers with far greater insight than a piece of work on its own and thus teachers can cater more effectively for each child's needs.
- Teachers look at the books every day and identify who needs support and who needs more challenge. They plan in targeted one-to-one or group conferences for the next day or session, or they hold spontaneous conferences and visualiser stops to address misconceptions or to extend thinking.
- During conference discussions, children are facilitated to identify their targets met and consider new ones. Conferences have replaced written marking. The marking is now live and in context.
- Teacher workload is reduced but their insight into children's learning and understanding is considerably increased. This insight then feeds back into assessment and planning.

Implementing change

The decisions we made along the way that are explored in the previous chapters will, I hope, help you to make Fast Feedback work in your own setting. Other examples, shared in this chapter, may help too. However, investing time and effort into creating a clear strategy, or plan for change, is key to minimising problems and to ensuring success. This chapter's fact file on implementing change can support in this should you want it.

Quick Tip: Knowing the theory around the effects of change on people can maximise the success of introducing Fast Feedback.

One of my favourite books of all time is *Our Iceberg is Melting* by John Kotter and Holger Rathgeber (2006), and I really recommend that you read this book about a penguin colony. Yes, I know I keep telling you to read all these books, but this one is truly the most entertaining and accessible metaphorical story on change that you'll ever read. Despite our mistakes and our need to tweak things, knowing some change theory did minimise our headaches.

FACT FILE: IMPLEMENTING CHANGE

What

Changes in education can result in new materials, behaviours, practices, understanding or the culture of the school itself. Implementing change effectively can be challenging, and change theory or change knowledge can be valuable for gaining support and getting results.

Why implementing change is important to Fast Feedback

Ending something that has been embedded in the culture of teaching for eons, like marking, could cause anxiety, resentment and other negative feelings that can affect the whole school. Fast Feedback is a huge change – but one for the better. Investing time and effort into creating a clear strategy or plan for implementing this approach can minimise problems for staff, children and families, and help to ensure the project's success.

Key people

- Michael Fullan – recognised internationally for his work on educational reform and his ideas for managing change; has written numerous books, including *The Six Secrets of Change* (2008).
- John Kotter – known for his ideas on change management and leadership; books include *Leading Change* (2012) and *Our Iceberg is Melting* (Kotter and Rathgeber, 2006).
- Tim Knoster – created the 'Knoster Model for Managing Complex Change' in 1991 (Knoster, 1991).

Key messages

Reactions to change

When faced with change, there can be resistance or negativity before a change is accepted.

The change curve (based on Kübler-Ross's Five Stages of Grief model, 1969)

Elizabeth Kübler-Ross was a psychiatrist who created a model to describe the stages of grief. Her model has since been adapted and is often referred to by business leaders and educationalists to provide insight into how people respond to change.

- Stage 1: Shock or denial – reality of a change hits:
  - Communication is key.

- Provide information and answer questions to support understanding.
- Give time to adjust.

- Stage 2: Concern, anger, resentment or fear (the danger zone) – may resist the change:
  - Plan and prepare carefully.
  - Pre-empt – consider the impact and objections.
  - Provide space to express concerns and vent anger.
  - Listen: address, minimise and mitigate problems.

- Stage 3: Acceptance (the turning point):
  - Give support and plenty of time to test what the change means.
  - Make sure all are well trained.
  - Build contingency time to learn and explore without pressure.

- Stage 4: Changes become second nature (improvements embraced) – see the benefits:
  - Team becomes productive and efficient.
  - Positive effects of change become apparent.
  - Celebrate the success.

Leading change effectively

Fullan, Kotter and Knoster offer models to help manage reactions to change and ensure that change is led and implemented effectively.

Fullan's six secrets of change (2016)

For large-scale or substantial change to be effective, there needs to be a theory of action. Fullan proposed six key components:

- Love your employees:
  - Build relationships, respect and regard; create a sense of camaraderie.
  - Enable development and provide motivational and meaningful work.
- Connect peers with purpose:
  - Facilitate peer interaction and build learning communities within and across schools.
  - Ensure staff are supported by leaders who enable knowledge to flow.
- Capacity building prevails:
  - Ensure teachers and leaders have the necessary instructional and change-management skills; continue to develop their competencies, resources and motivation.
  - Focus on the group and long-term goals and provide non-judgemental feedback.
- Learning is the work:
  - Provide opportunities for precise and personalised professional development.
  - Ensure the culture of the school promotes the continuous day-to-day learning of teachers, engaged in improving what they do.
- Transparency rules:
  - Provide ongoing data and access to effective practices.
  - Create a culture where it is normal to observe/be observed by coaches and mentors.

- Transparency, non-judgemental attitudes and good help result in classroom improvement.
- Systems learn:
  - Continuous learning depends on leaders and schools being confident in the face of complexity and in being open to new ideas.

Kotter's eight-step process of successful change

Kotter stresses the importance of not only thinking differently but also feeling differently for a more significant change in behaviour and results (Kotter and Rathgeber, 2006). Kotter's eight-step process can be used by leaders to gain support and propel change forward (Kotter, 2014). Below is a summarised version of the updated eight-step process (Kotter Inc, 2021).

1. Create a sense of urgency – *help others to see why change is needed, immediately.*
2. Build a guiding coalition – *assemble a group of effective people with skill to guide the change.*
3. Form a strategic vision and initiatives – *clarify the vision: how the future will be different and made a reality.*
4. Enlist a volunteer army – *ensure as many as possible understand and accept the vision.*
5. Enable action by removing barriers – *ensure these don't undermine the vision.*
6. Generate short-term wins – *collect visible successes as soon as possible to track progress and encourage persistence.*
7. Sustain acceleration – *press harder after initial successes; be relentless until the vision is a reality.*

8. Institute change – *connect new ways of behaving with successes; ensure they continue until they can replace old traditions.*

Why change can sometimes fail

Knoster's Model for Managing Complex Change

Knoster's model identifies key components for managing change; when there is an absence of just one component, change will not be implemented effectively.

Vision + Consensus + Skills + Incentive + Resources + Action plan = Change

- no vision (direction or bigger picture) = confusion
- no consensus (cooperation or collaboration) = negativity and sabotage
- no skills (expertise or capabilities) = anxiety
- no incentive (reasons or opportunities) = resistance
- no resources (physical or emotional) = frustration
- no action plan (steps, timescale or monitoring in place) = treadmill

A cultural change in the way things are done is required to achieve goals and success.

Putting it into practice

For leaders

- Conduct a trial and have those involved share what works so others can see for themselves.
- Plan carefully: create an action plan, pre-empt issues and share the vision. Why are we doing this? How does it fit?

- Ensure roles are delegated to the right people, even down to ordering the correct pens and resources!
- Listen to your staff and take on board their opinions; after all, they will be the ones putting it into action and they know their children best.
- Encourage staff to ask questions: have an open-door policy and a suggestion box for anonymous comments.
- Ensure plenty of time is given to 'iron out the creases' and be patient: it takes time for acceptance and change to become second nature.
- Use pupil voice: ask children to contribute their ideas and value their input.
- Be reflective and don't take things personally when there is resistance.
- Provide opportunities for peer learning and coaching, within and across different schools.
- Use the models and guides highlighted above to ensure change is implemented and managed effectively.

For teachers

- Ask questions: if you are not sure about something, it's likely others won't be either!
- Ask for clarity on the vision if you don't understand the need for change.
- Learn from peers and constructive feedback to build practice.
- Be champions for the change you want: don't be afraid to take ideas for change to leadership.
- Share the vision and reasons for change with your pupils so that they are fully informed and on board. They might have some interesting ideas too.

- Try not to become anxious and let leaders know if something isn't working: it takes time to adjust to change and find what works.

Key quote

'On the one hand, failing to act when the environment around you is radically changing leads to extinction. On the other hand, making quick decisions under conditions of mind-racing mania can be equally fatal.' (Fullan, 2020, p. ix)

Further reading

- Fullan, M. (2016), The six secrets of change – keynotes, https://michaelfullan.ca/wp-content/uploads/2016/06/2008SixSecretsofChangeKeynoteA4.pdf

  (For a simplified summary of his book (Fullan, 2008) and a brief insight into the work of others on change)
- Kotter, J. and Rathgeber, H. (2006), *Our Iceberg is Melting: Changing and Succeeding Under Any Conditions*. London: Macmillan.

  (For an easy, enjoyable read and more information about the eight steps towards successful change)

So, in terms of Kotter's steps, we already had our sense of urgency: the problem of teacher workload was (and still is!) well documented. Our penguin coalition team included leaders and teachers, and the trial and research out there helped us to create our strategic vision. What we didn't do properly was to enlist a sizeable 'army of volunteers'. We could have done this by increasing the number of classes involved in the trial, and possibly by extending the trial for a little longer. We would then have had a better range of adult and child feedback before whole-school roll-out.

Quick Tip: Consider involving a number of classes, across year groups and for an extended period of time, in your trial. This may put you in a better place to make the whole-school change.

Allowing our teachers to 'own' the project, by giving guidance and not restraints, helped to remove barriers to the change's success. However, as mentioned previously, although not marking saved hours for teachers, the 'loose guidance' added a different sort of workload and, for some, the 'quick wins' advised by Kotter were not so quick. Thus, our vision became blurred during the initial stages, and we had to give teachers that forum to share their worries and frustrations to get back on track. I have to say that sustaining the change, being relentless in driving it, was never in doubt, and Fast Feedback has most certainly replaced the tradition of writing in children's books.

Our written marking was replaced with live marking. I will mention here that our teachers told us that they found Fast Feedback quite physically demanding as they were moving around the classroom far more. They also admitted that they'd been tempted to 'use up' their saved hours by doing other school-related work, such as leadership tasks, revising planning and making more resources. Gemma stresses:

> *Yes, I did use up hours doing other school work, which felt worthwhile as it had such an impact on learning and progress. I did work less at the weekend though!* (Gemma)

These points are worth bearing in mind and such considerations will help your vision, and your path to it, to become clearer (and will also help you to get some penguins on board!).

Quick Tip: Making links with other no-marking schools to see how they managed the change will help you to ensure your process is successful.

Ways to trial and roll out Fast Feedback

So, what does Fast Feedback look like in other Ivy schools? As you know, Brimsdown Primary School carried out a trial at the same time as Lavender, and our non-negotiables and ensuing policies were very similar. Growth mindset training had taken place and 'resilience' had been added as a school value, but there were some key differences in rolling out Fast Feedback. We'll talk pen colour in a moment (of course) but one of the key differences was that Brimsdown didn't initially stop marking across the whole curriculum; instead, they started with just English and maths.

Should you decide to start smaller, the benefit is that staff and children will be able to get used to the new system before other subjects are added. Brimsdown then also trialled Fast Feedback in the foundation subjects before making it school-wide policy, which was a good idea. If you decide to take the same approach, remember that it does mean more change further down the line, which can impact on the systems already established. Lavender's 'all out' Fast Feedback was one big change, which we could establish and embed in the following months and years, but as you know that too has drawbacks. Whether it is better to do one big change event or two or three smaller ones will be something you'll want to consider carefully and consult with staff on. The approaches of two other Fast Feedback schools may help you to decide.

Churchfield and Larkspur Primary Schools became part of the Ivy Learning Trust (at different times) as they were failing schools. The new leadership teams had a lot to do but, despite the massive amount of work ahead of them, both teams saw an urgent need to introduce growth mindset and resilience (as detailed in Chapter 3). That happened before any thoughts of stopping marking were even entertained.

Quick Question: Do your children need the right mindset before you stop marking?

Once growth mindset was established and other issues addressed, Fast Feedback was introduced, but in quite different ways. Larkspur had been through turmoil for years. Ever-changing headship (each headteacher coming with new policies and practices) and plummeting results left a school whose parents had lost confidence, whose teachers and leaders felt lost and where pupil numbers were so low that the school was under threat of closure. The first thing the new leaders had to do was build morale. I was privileged to be part of that team in the early days, and our work around values, growth mindset and learning to learn happened quickly. Kerry (the headteacher) had an unwavering determination to gain the trust of the parents and to stabilise staff, systems and processes, which meant that Larkspur was eventually ready to trial no marking. It is a small school, so no marking was trialled first in just one year group (the Year 5 class) with Laura, who had come from Lavender. It was the obvious choice as she was already experienced in Fast Feedback. After the trial, Laura helped the senior leaders to establish no marking in other year groups. Year 6 wasn't included in the initial roll-out, due to other factors, but the rest of the school did Fast Feedback, first in English and maths and then in all other subjects.

> *It [Fast Feedback] really needs to be done in an RI [requires improvement] school. The dialogue is so much more powerful than the reams of nothingness.* (Kerry, Headteacher)

Churchfield took a slightly different approach. Nicky, the head, had come from Brimsdown and Natalie, the deputy, was the Natalie from Lavender (you know, the one way ahead of her time). Once all those issues that come with a failing school were on the road to recovery, they felt they were able to start their trial. The trial consisted of no marking in just maths but across the whole school. Afterwards, they did the same with English – a trial across the whole school. The findings from the two whole-school trials, and the training given before them, on metacognition and effective feedback, meant they could extend Fast Feedback to all subjects.

The point is that schools can introduce the change in different ways to suit their settings.

Quick Tip: Choose an approach to introducing Fast Feedback that suits your school, whether that be core subjects first, one subject at a time, or all at once. It has to be an approach that will work for your school, your staff, your children and your situation.

You may be trying to turn around a failing school and have a lot to do but, like the wrinkles, don't let a past grading put you off creating a great learning culture and reducing teacher workload.

You may be thinking that you'll stop marking in only one or two subjects alone, full stop, but trust me, once you understand the benefits of good, verbal feedback, the more ridiculous it seems to mark *anything*. Indeed, a recent discussion following a trial to reduce marking in one school led the teachers to wonder why they were marking at all, and to the leadership team thinking they might go back to the drawing board! Actually, it was this school that highlighted how difficult it would be for more experienced teachers to let go of the pen. All the no-marking schools have told me that these teachers found it hard at first. This message is consistent. Be prepared.

Different school approaches

OK, as I mentioned pens, I guess I'd better talk about colours. It doesn't matter! Or does it? Brimsdown have the 'Purple Pen of Power' and the 'Red Pen of Reflection', which I love. Other schools have other colours. What is interesting is that pens are very important to the children. Remember our little surveys? I can't tell you how many children commented on the pens when answering 'What don't you like?' or 'What can make Fast Feedback better?'. Here are some snippets:

The pens are a bit blobby.
The pens dry out when lids are left off.
A pot of spare pen lids would help.
Sometimes other children chew the pens (yuk).
We need our names on the pens.
It would be better if we used blue handwriting pens.
Can we have purple pens?
I love having the green pen. It's like I'm the teacher.

How you introduce 'no marking' to your school, what you call it and what colour pens you use (just don't forget to order them), will be for you to decide. Other elements too may be different.

For example, some no-marking schools continued to write in home reading records and to mark homework. Because they were still developing relationships with their families, these leaders believed it was important to maintain these forums for communication and home–school links. Some schools also decided to carry on using reward stickers in books, as they felt that many children still needed this type of feedback, and that growth mindset wasn't properly embedded. The decisions you make about these things will depend on where you are regarding aspects such as learning culture, community cohesion and what your own philosophical stance is.

Creating the right culture

All schools introduced growth mindset *before* trialling Fast Feedback. However, this wasn't the case with learning to learn. Where metacognition was developed *alongside* the no-marking roll-out, leaders told me that this impacted on the success of reflections and self-assessment. They then realised that learning to learn and metacognition strategies needed further work, or revisiting.

A few years ago, leaders from a teaching school alliance attended one of our professional conferences. They'd been given a grant to look at teacher workload and decided to base their research on the ideas around Fast Feedback. Jodie and I were invited to train their schools on growth mindset and learning to learn. At the presentation of their findings, however, the teachers said that they'd introduced 'live marking' too soon, that the children weren't ready and that they hadn't embedded the right mindset and learning culture. They thought that it was therefore not as effective as it could have been.

A very big tip

Developing the right culture (behaviour, questioning, peer work, meta-learning, mindset and so on) should, of course, continue during the trial and roll out of Fast Feedback, but it should be *introduced at least*, well before. In fact, I'd remind you of my comment at the end of Chapter 1: With the wrong culture, banning marking could be a disaster. But with the right culture, the impact is transformative. (Actually, even if you're not intending to go down the 'no-marking' route, creating the right learning culture can only be a good thing.)

Quick Question: What more do you need to do to develop your learning culture?

Further developing ownership

I must share with you a great strategy, introduced at some primary schools, to further develop a culture of learning ownership. Sorting books into piles, after a lesson, according to who might need a conference is a favourite strategy of teachers working in a Fast Feedback school. Another academy trust, that stopped marking around the same time as us, had a simple but even more effective idea, which also promoted self-assessment. At the end of the lesson, they got *their children* to place their books in one of three piles according to whether they found the work too easy, OK or whether they needed some help. A small move, yet the knowledge that each teacher gains from this simple action is huge. The teacher is, yet again, inside a child's head, understanding how that child sees themselves in relation to the task and the learning, even if it's in the wrong pile. One teacher at Lavender, who also used this system, highlights:

> *I had a GD [greater depth] child who always went for the middle pile, even when it was correct. I also had lower-achieving children who said they were secure when they clearly weren't. It identified, for me, who needed more support with metacognition and mindset.* (Year 6 teacher)

One Ivy school uses a similar strategy, with a 'conference box' available for children to pop their book into if they feel they need help with something.

Quick Tip: For even more insight, ask children to put their book into one of three piles at the end of the lesson according to whether the work was hard, easy or just right.

Teacher to teacher

As well as piling books, Fast Feedback teachers will, of course, make notes. I spoke before about how those new to no marking will often write reams of notes at the beginning, but will eventually develop their *own* time-efficient systems. This is the case in other no-marking schools too, where teachers do their record-keeping differently. It doesn't matter how they do this (leaders are looking at children's progress, not teacher notes, remember), as long as the system works to better the children's learning.

Nothing highlights the need for freedom of choice over this more than the case of job-sharing teachers Katie (the one who was really anxious in the last chapter) and Sarah. They created systems and strategies that would ensure smooth transition and shared knowledge. Katie highlights, from a part-time, job-share perspective, how positive the change was:

> *Before Fast Feedback, sharing information after marking, late on a Thursday night, with Sarah, who taught (and conferenced) first thing on a Friday morning, was difficult to say the least. Using our own system of assessment and recording when we'd stopped marking not only saved hours of time, but also meant a much smoother transition between us. Of course, we also had far more insight into where the children were in terms of their learning!* (Katie, Year 5 teacher)

Katie and Sarah developed a range of record sheets over that first year, which differed depending on the subject or activity. Figure 7.1 shows an example that follows a Big Writing session. As you can see, it gives the 'at a glance' information needed to carry out effective one-to-one or group conferences.

It's simple. Instead of Katie talking through each child's performance with Sarah at 7.00 am on a Friday morning, she could hand over the notes with a quick, more general discussion.

Handing over to other teachers doesn't have to be difficult with no marking. In fact, Fast Feedback systems can make teacher transition easier in a number of ways. I spoke with Margarita, a supply/cover teacher, who used to teach at both Lavender and Brimsdown Schools. I asked her if it had been difficult for her to switch, as we had slightly different systems (and pen colours). She reminded me that the philosophy is the same. The children were so in charge of their learning that they were able to explain the system to her, if necessary. She also said that the quick note-taking and piling of books saved her hours of marking too, something much appreciated. The other thing she valued was being invited to all the staff training so that she understood the theory behind the practice.

Figure 7.1 *Grouping children by 'conference need' is an efficient and effective way to hand over to job shares or cover teachers.*

Quick Tip: Ensure that all members of staff, including class teachers, teaching assistants, cover staff and leaders, are trained when introducing Fast Feedback.

Fast Feedback for all children

Support staff at Lavender say they have benefited from having INSET on questioning, growth mindset and metacognition as they are able to support the pedagogy when working with groups and individuals. One-to-one learning support assistants and intervention staff understand how Fast Feedback works and have been able to adapt or resource it for the children they work with who may have special needs, or for those very new to English.

Many of our conference questions have been around how to get children with different needs to mark their own work or to reflect on their learning. One of the benefits of joining an Ivy professional conference is that you get to walk around the schools and see Fast Feedback in action. What you will see is children marking and reflecting, with the level of support that they need, as you would see with *any* learning activity. LSAs can be highly creative and will work alongside teachers to meet the vast range of different children's needs. When asked about the learning, if a child can communicate their feelings with just a facial expression, they have still shared a reflection. They are involved. In terms of children new to English, if a child needs visuals or an interpreter to help them find the right vocabulary to express how they got on with their learning, they are still sharing. Every approach may be different, but there is no reason to exclude any child from thinking about and having some ownership of their learning.

Fast Feedback with the very young

Questions are often raised about Early Years as well. How can very young children mark their own work and write reflections? It is so important to start children on this path from a young age. Children in nursery and Reception classes are encouraged to talk about what they have learned, how they felt about the activity and, eventually, what they might like to do to make it even better next time.

Figure 7.2 shows two examples from the same Reception child (the child's words have been scribed by an adult). We have the very first piece of writing done in his book and you can see that the reflection is simple and general. The second shows how, by the summer term, he is thinking about specific successes and is even ready to talk about how to move his learning on.

Figure 7.2 *Over the course of a year, when asked about their work, this Reception child's reflections became less general and far more about learning.*

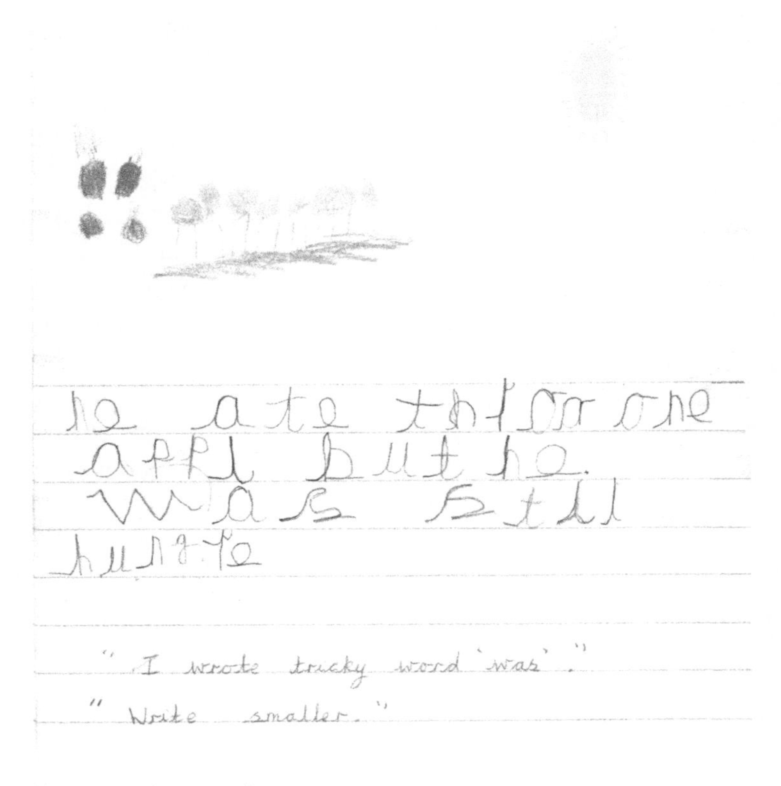

Figure 7.2 *(continued)*

Quick Tip: Having an adult scribe a child's words for them when talking about their learning means that the written record can then be referred to the next time that child is reflecting on their work.

Ideally, as children start to mark-make and ascribe meaning, they can be encouraged to write their own evaluations, having been given verbal cues or sentence starters, and then tell their friends or adults what the reflection says. Bear in mind, however, that for very young children especially, the physical act of writing can be very tiring!

The key message is that the skills of learning and ownership should start when they're young. It may not be so easy for your teachers to develop those skills with little ones at first, but it will certainly make more sense to them than writing things that children can't read in 30 books. This is what Laura had to say about her first experience of Fast Feedback as a Year 1 teacher:

> *I remember my treat after Big Marking on a Friday. At about 7.00 pm, I'd get changed in the school toilets so I could go to the pub with a colleague. Fast Feedback was tricky at first. I devised a carousel system to do group reflections so that the children could talk about their learning. English was easier than maths: we'd work through the toolkit together so that children could say what they wanted to tick and why. In maths, I'd have to work harder to unpick their reasoning. It's all just gentle guidance really and so much better than marking books. Plus, I could go home to get changed for the pub!* (Laura, Year 1 teacher)

Fast Feedback beyond primary school?

The approaches that schools, and even individual teachers, take when stopping marking may have to differ according to age, need, setting, learning culture and many other factors. One size doesn't fit all but the benefits of verbal feedback most certainly do. It's worth noting that many secondary school colleagues have attended our professional conferences with a view to introducing certain elements of Fast Feedback to older pupils.

It would be fitting to share with you now some thoughts from Lavender children who have lived their whole primary school lives with Fast Feedback. Unfortunately, we're not quite there yet. However, at the time of writing, the Year 6 children heading off to secondary school have been writing reflections and having conferences since they were in Year 2. I spoke to a couple of average-ability children at the end of the term, using some questions from the old questionnaire. Let's see what they said.

> ***Who is in charge of your learning?*** *Us. It's not the teacher's fault if you don't focus on your learning.*
>
> ***What helps you to be a good learner?*** *You have to take advantage of good teachers. Use resources and try your best. Listen, be determined and keep trying. You'll get it eventually. Hear other people's point of view.*
>
> ***How do you feel about writing reflections after your work?*** *It shows if we understood. I like doing them after role-play in drama because it helps me understand what we've done. We can read other people's reflections for ideas on what things to write.*
>
> ***How do you feel about cooperative reviews?*** *It's a chance to understand from a friend's point of view, especially if their writing is better.*

It struck me that they would now have to get used to seeing teachers' writing in their books and I asked them about this. One said a smiley face might be nice... but she knew that words were more effective (bless her). The other said that when she marks her own work, she keeps looking at it and making it better, but she would probably still do that.

So, children *can* self-regulate and become effective learners for life. And teachers *can* have a life. But why stop there? The benefits of Fast Feedback for children are immense, but I'd like to bring the story back to the original reason behind Matthew's idea, that of teacher wellbeing. First, let's have our quick recap:

Chapter Summary

- Change has to be carefully planned if it is to be successful.
- There is no one way to trial and roll out Fast Feedback.
- Different elements can be changed to suit your setting.
- The right learning culture must be created before Fast Feedback is introduced.
- All children should be included in the Fast Feedback approach.
- Fast Feedback leads to lifelong learners.

8 It's not over yet *Next steps in the Fast Feedback journey*

Reduce the stress

Before the introduction of Fast Feedback at Lavender, we'd already put in place initiatives to reduce stress and promote staff wellbeing. We had a wellbeing team that met to discuss issues and organise fabulous feel-good events, and we had 'secret friends' leaving chocolate frogs in different people's pigeon-holes. Once Mr Appreciation had joined our values team, staff and children could fill in and hand out appreciation cards to one another, as a 'thank you' (my most treasured was from a Year 6 child who struggled with behaviour, thanking me for a lunchtime detention – seriously!).

We also introduced our 'green grass' box. This came about because a teacher left Lavender and later told me they'd regretted the decision and that the 'grass wasn't greener'. Perhaps things weren't better in other schools, but Lavender still had work to do around teacher retention and wellbeing. So, I covered a paper box with grass-print vinyl, made a hole in the top, popped it in the staff room and invited comments and suggestions to make Lavender's grass as green as possible. All right, all right, it's just a suggestion box, but it helped us to improve many different aspects of school life.

Quick Tip: Leaders, if like us you decide to invite anonymous suggestions, don't waste angst-ridden hours trying to work out who wrote what!

Then, of course, we had Fast Feedback. However, our communication still needed work (whose doesn't?) so we asked Sarah, a very positive leader, to share details of the week's coming events during staff meetings in her most chirpy manner. This she did, along with a 'fascinating fact' for added positivity. It was both useful *and* fun.

We thought we were somewhat special (another smug alert), until she announced one week, *'And of course, be nice to Year 5 next week as it's their monitoring week. If you see them looking a bit down or stressed, offer to help, or give them an extra smile…'*

Bam! It hit me! What on Earth are we doing? We are putting teachers through something so awful that we need to announce 'be kind' to them at a staff meeting. Where does that sit in the wellbeing, workload agenda? Jodie and I spoke. We both knew that something had to change.

Lesson observations

I think back to my own class teacher days and how I felt when an observation was imminent. I hated it. My credibility as a professional depended on the opinion of one or two leaders judging my every move, and the reaction of the children to my every move, in a fixed amount of time, on a specified day. I'd spend hours planning and resourcing that one lesson. I'd be anxious before (what will they think?), anxious during (what are they thinking?), and anxious afterwards (what did they think?). How would I be 'graded'?

Ofsted did well getting rid of grades back then. We did the same; we 'triangulated', we spoke to children, we took in the books (for scrutiny), we sandwiched the feedback (good, bad, good). None of that stopped the anxiety, the build-up and the stress. Comments afterwards, such as 'if only you'd come yesterday' or 'if only you'd stayed for another ten minutes', were common. I've said them myself.

Quick Question: Are formal observations at your school stressful? For teachers? For support staff? For leaders?

The idea that praise and support plans were based on one formal lesson observation a term was a nonsense. Invariably, the teacher had spent days meticulously planning and resourcing the 'best-ever lesson', so how could you really 'know' their day-to-day teaching? Some teachers would be so worried that they'd take extreme actions: I know of one teacher who would leave a big box of chocolates on her desk during an observation. She'd sweetly say to the children just before the observation, 'Let's see how well behaved you are.' Bribery aside, if an observation lesson 'goes wrong', as a leader you still don't know how the teaching is day to day. One-off, termly observations are not reliable indicators of teacher performance.

So, what is an observation for? What really matters when considering a teacher's performance? Is it the perfect one-hour 'show' once a term? Of course not. All we really want to see is children engaged in learning. Sometimes they'll be entertained, sometimes they'll have their heads down, sometimes they'll be in deep discussion with an adult or peer. How do we know they're learning? Because the books tell us. The children tell us. The teacher will sometimes instruct, sometimes test, sometimes facilitate and, yes, sometimes entertain. But this shouldn't be for the benefit of an observer; it should be to create an effective learning experience for the children at that time.

Peer evaluation, CPD and performance management

Thankfully, we were already on the path towards a more meaningful, less stressful way to manage performance and to develop staff. We had introduced a project whereby teachers were encouraged to video themselves teaching and then critique their own practice against specific developmental points. (This is fascinating, by the way. If you've never done it, I highly recommend you do. It's amazing what you see – once you get past what you look or sound like.) Also, before Fast Feedback, Jodie had introduced Lesson Study across the school, where teachers were peer-evaluating the learning happening in each other's classrooms and planning together to address gaps.

Thanks to the work of Liz, an assistant head some years before, our performance management policy had long been linked to the learning of children identified *with* the teacher during discussions at pupil progress meetings. Our CPD was a good mix of teacher-led, whole-staff, teacher- or TA/LSA-focused, self-choice workshops and leadership training. But formal lesson observations were not in line with our learning culture.

Fast Feedback for teachers

Fast Feedback was embedded for our children. They were having regular discussions around their learning and were getting instant pointers to improve their practice. The next step in our journey seemed obvious. If we were giving Fast Feedback to the children, we should give it to the adults too. We should ditch formal lesson observations completely and… helicopter!

Learning walks

Being a national support school meant that our teachers were used to people popping in to 'have a look' anyway, so we introduced open-door 'learning walks'. Pairs of leaders (subject/middle leaders included) could drop in on a lesson, spend no more than five minutes observing or chatting with children, and take a few pertinent notes. To begin with, we fed back to the teachers (and support staff) verbally, at the soonest opportunity. Where this wasn't possible, we used written postcards as a back-up. We eventually sent emails, as teachers wanted them for their professional development folders; however, a face-to-face conversation was always encouraged, where proper dialogue around teaching and learning could take place. Like the drop-ins, any written feedback was informal, friendly and developmental. Here's an example:

> *Hi Millie,*
>
> *We enjoyed popping into your science lesson today – thank you. We loved the activity and how well-planned your questioning was. I did notice that J wasn't as engaged as she might have been. Might be something to watch for? It would be great to chat about this, or anything else, if you want to. Just catch me at lunchtime, or we can make a different time that's suitable for you.*

In the beginning, a few staff were wary of regular learning walks, and said it would feel like having observations every week. However, we made it clear that this was about wellbeing and professional development, not about *more* monitoring and certainly not about judging. They understood the vision. They understood that this approach would give a far more realistic picture of their day-to-day teaching and reduce the stress around 'big' observations. Learning walks became a way of life. Leaders share their 'walk' findings and together they identify how support will be given, what excellence can be shared and whether there are whole-school threads that need to be addressed. They don't spend hours watching one-off lessons and writing notes about them. It's less stress for teachers but also for leaders – who have more time to come up with innovative ideas!

What's mine is yours

So, whose idea is Fast Feedback? Who owns 'no marking', 'live marking', 'verbal marking', 'minimal marking' and all the other names you can think of? When Matthew had the idea to ban marking at Lavender (though I've heard it may have been Tina, his wife's, idea), that doesn't mean that someone else hadn't already been thinking about doing the exact same thing – or indeed was *doing* that very same thing. Whilst writing this book, memories came flooding back and one of them was of a course I'd attended back in 2012. I remember another delegate telling me that her school 'didn't mark' and I was horrified. Schools across the country may have reduced or stopped marking long before Lavender did, or at the same time, or after; it doesn't matter. Any of us might have read the great theories and ideas of those mentioned throughout this book and followed the same path at the same time. The story of how marking was banned at Lavender belongs to Lavender, but the Fast Feedback idea isn't owned by anyone. The only conversation to be had around ownership is that of learning.

Hopefully, this book will have given you some ideas on how you can promote that ownership of learning, and reduce teacher workload, through Fast Feedback. If you want more information and guidance, I would recommend that you attend one of Ivy's professional conferences, where you'll have the chance to see Fast Feedback in action. I promise this isn't shameless selling, as I have nothing to gain personally from you attending, but you will gain more insight. You will watch teachers giving feedback through conferencing, and you can look in children's books and ask them about their reflections and their learning. I won't pretend that you'll walk into a perfect school (well, you might) but, as with this book, you will get an honest picture.

To give you an example, at our second professional conference I'd decided, at the last minute, to invite children to come and speak to the audience. Gemma and I chose three Year 6 children who wouldn't be too terrified to speak in front of a whole bunch of teachers and leaders. Well, they were *slightly* terrified but still wanted to do it: the fear of failure or embarrassment was far less than the anticipation of a new and exciting challenge. We had done well (yep, smug). We asked them to quickly plan something to say about Fast Feedback, the good points, bad points and so on. We wanted honesty. J was visibly shaking, but spoke out beautifully:

'Another thing I really like about Fast Feedback is that my book is so much neater now the teachers don't write in it any more…'

It got a laugh.

But what does this really say? For me, it says that writing in children's books day after day, night after night for no good reason can be a messy business. A wearisome messy business. A stressful messy business.

I will end now on a serious note, which confirms this. Someone I know, who works in a primary school, overheard a teacher say to a child (in a very stressed and cross voice):

> *'Well, what's the point of me writing in your book if you don't even read it!?'*

Cut the nonsense.

Increase the learning.

Keep your teachers.

(Wheely suitcases are for holidays.)

References

Anderson, L. W. and Krathwohl, D. R. (2001), *A Taxonomy for Teaching, Learning and Assessing: A Revision of Bloom's Taxonomy of Educational Objectives*. New York: Longman.

Berger, R. (2018), Here's what's wrong with Bloom's Taxonomy: A deeper learning perspective, Education Week, www.edweek.org/education/opinion-heres-whats-wrong-with-blooms-taxonomy-a-deeper-learning-perspective/2018/03

Bjork, R. A. and Bjork, E. L. (2020), 'Desirable difficulties in theory and practice', *Journal of Applied research in Memory and Cognition*, 9, (4), 475–479.

Bloom, B. S. (1956), *Taxonomy of Educational Objectives: The Classification of Educational Goals. Handbook I: Cognitive Domain*. New York: David McKay Company.

Blosser, P. E. (1975), *How to Ask the Right Questions*. Arlington: National Science Teachers Association.

Building Learning Power (BLP) (2018a), Creating learning friendly classroom cultures, www.buildinglearningpower.com/2018/05/creating-metacognitive-classroom-cultures

Building Learning Power (BLP) (2018b), The Learning Power Equation, www.buildinglearningpower.com

Cameron, J. and Pierce, W. D. (1994), 'Reinforcement, reward and intrinsic motivation: A meta-analysis', *Review of Educational Research*, 64, (3), 363–423.

Clarke, S. (2008), *Active Learning Through Formative Assessment*. London: Hodder Education.

Clarke, S. (2021), *Unlocking Learning Intentions and Success Criteria*. USA: Corwin.

Claxton, G. (2002), *Building Learning Power: Helping Young People Become Better Learners*. Bristol: TLO Ltd.

Claxton, G. (2018), *The Learning Power Approach: Teaching Learners to Teach Themselves*. Carmarthen: Crown House Publishing.

Claxton, G. (2021), *The Future of Teaching and the Myths That Hold It Back*. Oxon: Routledge.

Corbett, P. (2021), Explore and download Talk for Writing resources for free, www.talk4writing.com/resources

Deci, E. L., Koestner, R. and Ryan, R. M. (2001), 'Extrinsic rewards and intrinsic motivation in education: Reconsidered once again', *Review of Educational Research*, 71, (1), 1–27.

Department for Education (2014), National Curriculum, www.gov.uk/government/collections/national-curriculum

Durran, J. (2019), Re-thinking 'success criteria': A simple device to support pupils' writing, https://jamesdurran.blog/2019/01/24/re-thinking-success-criteria-a-simple-device-to-support-pupils-writing

Dweck, C. S. (2006), *Mindset: The New Psychology of Success*. New York: Random House.

Dweck, C. S. (2014), The power of believing that you can improve, TED, www.ted.com/talks/carol_dweck_the_power_of_believing_that_you_ can_improve

Dweck, C. S. (2017), *Mindset: Changing The Way You Think to Fulfil Your Potential* (updated edition). New York: Random House.

Dweck, C. and Gross-Loh, C. (2016), How praise became a consolation prize, *The Atlantic*, www.theatlantic.com/education/archive/2016/12/how-praise-became-a-consolation-prize/510845

Education Endowment Foundation (EEF) (2018), Teaching and Learning Toolkit: Feedback, https://educationendowmentfoundation.org.uk/evidence-summaries/teaching-learning-toolkit/feedback

Education Endowment Foundation (EEF) (2020), Metacognition and self-regulated learning: Learning guidance report: Seven recommendations for teaching self-regulated learning & metacognition, https://educationendowmentfoundation.org.uk/tools/guidance-reports/metacognition-and-self-regulated-learning

E L Education (2012), Austin's Butterfly: Building excellence in student work, https://vimeo.com/38247060

Fullan, M. (2008), *The Six Secrets of Change*. San Francisco: Jossey-Bass.

Fullan, M. (2016), The six secrets of change – keynotes, https://michaelfullan.ca/wp-content/uploads/2016/06/2008SixSecretsofChangeKeynoteA4.pdf

Fullan, M. (2020), *Leading in a Culture of Change* (2nd edition). San Francisco: Jossey Bass.

Gilbert, I. (2007), *The Little Book of Thunks*. Carmarthen: Crown House Publishing.

Gladwell, M. (2006), *Blink: The Power of Thinking Without Thinking*. London: Penguin.

Hattie, J. A. C. (2009), *Visible Learning: A Synthesis of 800+ Meta-Analyses on Achievement*. Oxon: Routledge.

Hattie, J. (2012), *Visible Learning for Teachers: Maximizing Impact on Learning*. Oxon: Routledge.

Hattie, J. (2021), Visible Learning: What works best for learning, https://visible-learning.org

Hattie, J. and Clarke, S. (2019), *Visible Learning: Feedback*. Oxon: Routledge.

Hattie, J. and Timperley, H. (2007) 'The power of feedback', *Review of Educational Research*, 77, (1), 81–112.

House of Commons Education Committee (2017), Recruitment and retention of teachers, https://publications.parliament.uk/pa/cm201617/cmselect/cmeduc/199/199.pdf

Independent Teacher Workload Review Group (2016), Eliminating unnecessary workload around marking, https://assets.publishing.service.gov.uk/government/uploads/system/uploads/attachment_data/file/511256/Eliminating-unnecessary-workload-around-marking.pdf

Killian, S. (2015), An objective critique of Hattie's Visible Learning research, Australian Society for Evidence Based Teaching, www.evidencebasedteaching.org.au/wp-content/uploads/An-Objective-Critique-of-Hatties-Visible-Learning-Research.pdf

Knoster, T. (1991), 'Managing complex change', TASH conference, Washington DC, June, 1991 (adapted by Knoster from Enterprise Group Ltd).

Kotter, J. (2012), *Leading Change*. Boston: Harvard Business Review Press.

Kotter, J. (2014), *Accelerate: Building a Strategic Agility for a Fast-Moving World*. Boston: Harvard Business Review Press.

Kotter Inc (2021), The 8 step process for leading change, www.kotterinc.com/8-step-process-for-leading-change

Kotter, J. and Rathgeber, H. (2006), *Our Iceberg is Melting: Changing and Succeeding Under Any Conditions*. London: Macmillan.

Kübler-Ross, E. (1969), *On Death and Dying*. New York: Macmillan.

Kulik, J. A. and Kulik, C.-I. C. (1988), 'Timing of feedback and verbal learning', *Review of Educational Research*, 58, (1), 79–97.

Lepper, M. R., Greene, D. and Nisbett, R. E. (1973), 'Undermining children's intrinsic interest with extrinsic reward: A test of the "overjustification" hypothesis', *Journal of Personality and Social Psychology*, 28, (1), 129–137.

Mindset Works (2017), The impact of a growth mindset, www.mindsetworks.com/Science/Impact

Minkel, J. (2015), Distracted by rewards: Moving beyond carrots and sticks, Education Week, www.edweek.org/teaching-learning/opinion-distracted-by-rewards-moving-beyond-carrots-and-sticks/2015/03

Musical Playground, School Values Song, www.youtube.com/watch?v=MSPXA3nklxA

Ofsted (2016), School report: Brimsdown Primary School, https://files.ofsted.gov.uk/v1/file/2593853

Ofsted (2020), School report: Inspection of a good school: Lavender Primary School, https://files.ofsted.gov.uk/v1/file/50145344

Pink, D. H. (2018), *Drive: The Surprising Truth About What Motivates Us*. Edinburgh: Cannongate.

Revised Bloom's Taxonomy Action Verbs, www.apu.edu/live_data/files/333/blooms_taxonomy_action_verbs.pdf

Ryan R. M. and Deci, E. L. (2000), Self-determination theory and the facilitation of intrinsic motivation, social development, and well-being, https://selfdeterminationtheory.org/SDT/documents/2000_RyanDeci_SDT.pdf

School 21, Beautiful work, www.school21.org.uk/beautiful-work

Shirley Clarke Education (2021a), Formative assessment: A summary, https://www.shirleyclarke-education.org/what-is-formative-assessment

Shirley Clarke Education (2021b), Transforming learning through formative assessment, www.shirleyclarke-education.org

Skinner, B. F. (1938), *The Behavior of Organisms: An Experimental Analysis*. New York: Appleton-Century.
Skinner, B. S. (1953), *Science and Human Behavior*. New York: Macmillan.
Smith, I. (2007), *Asking Better Questions*. Cambridge: Learning Unlimited.
Smith, J. (2017), *The Lazy Teacher's Handbook: How Your Students Learn More When You Teach Less* (new edition). Carmarthen: Crown House Publishing.
Sutton, R. M., Hornsey, M. J. and Douglas, K. M. (eds) (2012), *Feedback: The Communication of Praise, Criticism and Advice*. New York: Peter Lang US.
Syed, M. (2011), *Bounce: The Myth of Talent and the Power of Practice*. London: Fourth Estate.
Vygotsky, L. (1962), *Thought and Language*. Cambridge, MA: MIT Press.
Willingham, D. T. (2007), Ask the cognitive scientist: Should learning be its own reward? AFT, www.aft.org/ae/winter2007-2008/willingham
Wilson, R. (2012), *Big Writing: Writing Voice and Basic Skills* (new edition). Oxford: Oxford University Press.

Index